SUCCESS & WEALTH
THROUGH THE BIBLE

Lungelo Shandu

Scripture quotations taken from CONTEMPORARY ENGLISH
VERSION BIBLE, Copyrights © 1995 by American Bible Society.

Scripture quotations taken from the AMPLFIED BIBLE, Copyright
© 1954, 1958, 1962, 1964, 1965, 1987 by The Lockman Foundation.
All rights reserved. Used by permission. (www.Lockman.org)

First edition 2015 by Kwarts Publishers

ISBN: 978-1-77605-079-6

DEDICATION

This book is dedicated to **believers** who desire to live life without any limitations. I'm here to show you how everything is possible when you believe. As much as I have used the Bible during my research, I find it to be the greatest motivational book; everyone can relate to it whether they are Christians or not. The book is meant to inspire you and to change your life forever.

I have also used other forms of research and I have come to realise that there is this formula; one that all successful people who have lived on this earth before and the ones that are still alive agree upon when it comes to living life without limits. And I'm here to reveal the secret that they have been using in private and over the years to make themselves successful and be where they are today.

CONTENTS

ABOUT THE AUTHOR

Lungelo Shandu is a 28 year male convict. I am the first born of two in the marriage of my parents. I was born in the township called Umlazi N section and moved to KwaMashu P section when I was two years old. I have Matric and also continued with my studies in Business Management during my term of incarceration and I obtain an N5 qualification. I am single and also the father of three girls.

During my term of incarceration I have a lot of time to observe everything regarding life and I also equipped myself with a lot of information. I then saw a gap to be filled in, and also a way to give back to the community of the world by sharing my knowledge that I have gathered over the years; which will also assist you in changing your life and taking it to the next level.

Over the past years I have made a lot of terrible decisions which led me to be in prison. Through the challenges I am facing during my incarceration, I came to realise that I have been creating everything that has ever happened in my life, and I was unconscious as I was creating everything.

Since I came to realisation of the power that I have within me, I made another decision of being in control of my life and this time I am conscious regarding everything that I do. All the decisions that I made brought change in my life and since I am creating my future with a conscious mind, I have been receiving abundance of success and it keeps on flowing in my life, and now is the time to share it with you. I'm here to show you on how to pursue this life journey we are on. I am a first time Author who tells the naked truth about life and how it's supposed to be lived while you achieve every desire you have ever dreamt off.

ACKNOWLEDGEMENT

To Khanyisile Zuma thank you for your support and wanting me to grow as a person. Without you this book was not going to be possible. To Phumalni Mngomezulu thank you for assisting me further and answering all my questions whenever I needed advice and guidance. And to all my prison mates Isaiah (Sge) Lunga, Bonginkosi Majola, Jack Gumede, Nkululeko Ntenza - thank you guys for availing yourselves whenever I needed advice on how to move forward and discuss the book in the early stages. You all believed in me and kept pushing me. And again I would like to send a special thank you to Jack Gumede for taking his precious time and assisting me on editing the book.

In life nothing happens by chance. Everything is part of our journey and as you are holding this book, you created this day for yourself and your journey should change for the best from now onwards. Thank you so much to everyone who is reading this book and I promise that the book will be helpful if you follow its instructions. And most importantly all my help in putting this book together comes from the Lord God, and all the glory, honour and praise belongs to Him.

INTRODUCTION

In this book I will show you how to use what God has given you to get anything and everything that you have ever desired in your whole entire life. I will show you the quickest way with no waiting period to get or be anything you want to be. I will be showing you with proof that God has already given you everything you have ever wished for, and the only thing you need to do is to step forward and meet God half way so you can discover your talents and gifts that are within you right now, and how to use them to your fullest ability.

If you gave someone special an expensive gift and that person doesn't use that gift at all, how would you feel? I would personally feel sad, disappointed and angry; and surely you would feel the same way too. The same thing applies to God, He has given us many different talents and He wants us to use them to our fullest abilities. If we don't use them at all, He won't be happy with us and even if we use 50% of our talents, He would still be angry because it will show Him that we don't appreciate what He has given us.

That's why in this book I will show you exactly what to do through the Bible, and use what you have right now, which is your **mind**, **emotions** and your **voice**. I will show you how you can heal your life, heal your relationships, be successful, be wealthy, get rich, live your dream life and be or do anything you have ever wished to do or be; through the Bible, God's Word. That's what God wants from us, to be and have all our desires and serve Him truthfully.

Once you have mastered what I will tell you in full details, you will find life very easy and every good thing will be coming your way anywhere you are. Yes I said it, anywhere you are right now. And you will live the life you have always dreamt off. If you follow this book accordingly to what I have said through the Bible, failure is not even an option, but only abundance of wealth and success is going to come to you where you are right now. God has blessed me with the knowledge and He wants me to pass it on to you using His Word, so you can up lift your life right away.

He has heard your cries, pain and suffering in your prayers and since you are reading this book right now; He wants to answer your prayers right away. By purchasing this book you have already taken the first step in changing your life. If you have faith, a believer and believe in the Bible, you will find everything very easy to understand in this book. And even if you don't believe in the Bible, you have come to the right book since everything you need to use is currently within you right now.

No matter which religious group you come from or you don't even go to church, you will still find this book relevant, helpful and you will enjoy it. You must make it your best friend from now onwards because it will make you successful, wealthy and bring all your desires and happiness straight to you **now without any delays**!

The first chapter is the foundation of the whole book and it tells and shows where the power to be successful and wealthy comes from. The following chapters teach you how the power can be used till you get all your desires and live your dream world. The second last chapter **do not** have anything to say from the Bible, but it's the summary of everything I have said from the previous chapters. All chapters will include some headings of the previous or following chapters since everything that is said on this book works together and cannot be separated. Nevertheless, I'm sure you would agree with me when I say the Bible consist of 66 books that were written by real people. All those people spoke one thing in common and they spoke these things through God's Word. And it's also true that the Bible has much to say to help us deal with the issues confronting us today. Another thing that most people don't know is that the Bible is the greatest source of motivation, and I'm going to prove to you as you continue to read the whole book.

It's also true that Jesus Christ was born just like me and you so he could show us the way to life and the way to live. Now in the book of John 14:12 Jesus said, "I tell you for certain that if you have faith in me, you will do the same things that I am doing. You will do even greater things, now that I am going back to the father."

Now this verse clearly states everything and I will explain it to you further as you continue to read. We need to start in the beginning in order to get to this verse and understand it clearly. Therefore, all my life I have believed that the Bible is written in a way that things are hidden inside it and you need to have Holy Spirit inside you so you can understand it. I'm sure some of you still believe that even now. You have the same Spirit that Jesus Christ has right now inside of you as I speak.

From now onwards you will understand the Bible clearly and what God expert from us; and not only that, you will enjoy reading the Bible and listening to God's Word. Let's start now and let me take you through this amazing life changing journey and be, and have everything you have ever desired in your whole life.

Chapter 1

WHO ARE YOU AND WHAT POWERS DO YOU HAVE?

We as people must stop looking at things as they were things that were happening long time ago, because all the things they are talking about in the Bible are the things that are happening in this current time. The Bible was written so that it will equip us for our life's journey. Now let me show you in this book on how to use the Bible to your fullest ability and be successful and wealthy today! In order for you to understand this whole book and use it to your full advantage, we have to start somewhere first and clarify some few points which are the basics.

Now who am I really?

2Corinthians 5:1, our bodies are like tents that we live in here on this earth. When these tents are destroyed God will give us a place to live. Then who am I if I am like a tent which is going to be destroyed one day? Is there someone living inside me if I will continue to live after the tent has been destroyed? And who is God that will give me a place to live after my tent has been destroyed? Now these are the questions I know some of you are asking yourselves. The answer is simple, and it's all in the Bible that you have at home or with you now. If you have a Bible with you right now, come on and let's check the answers on the scriptures that I'm going to giving you. If you don't have a Bible with you right now, you can check it later as soon as you have access to it. But for now I will give you the answers you are looking for.

In the book of John 4:24, it clearly states that God is a Spirit. Now wait, in the book of Genesis 1:27 it tells us that God created humans to be like Himself. Since God is a Spirit and He created humans to be like Him, does that mean that I am like God and I am a Spirit?

Now if God is a Spirit and He made me to be like Himself that means I am a Spirit. So what is a Spirit really? The Spirit is the power inside you, the power to perform action. Just like your biological father, after he was intimate with your mother, you were born and you had everything that your father has. You got ears, nose, mouth, legs, hands and the list is endless, but you have all these body parts just like him so you can use them like he does. So if he was a mechanic that means you can also be a mechanic if you pursue that direction because he gave you the tools he also uses to do the job of mechanic. And those tools are the hands.

Just like God, since He is a Spirit and He created humans to be like Himself that means we have every tool we need to do and perform every action we want to do just like Him, because He is our Father who created us to be just like Himself. He gave us the tool to do all the things He does.

But now, how did I get the tools to do all the things He does because God is a Spirit? In the book of Genesis 2:7, it tells us that God breathed life into the man, and the man started breathing. That is how we got the Spirit and the tool to use and perform action with it. So it is true that we are Spirits because the man breathed after God had breathed life into him.

So if He breathed life what did He really give me? The meaning of the word "LIFE" means to give somebody vitality, and "vitality" means physical and mental energy, and "energy" means power, and "power" means the ability to do, and "do" means perform action. I am breaking down everything and every word step by step because I need us to stay on the same page here, since this is one of the most important part of the book.

So everything adds up now, God gave me the power to perform action. And since God is a Spirit and breathed life into me that means I have the power inside me right now; the power to perform any action. Now let's look in the book of 1 Corinthians 3:16, it says you are God's temple and His Spirit lives inside you. So now it makes sense when 2 Corinthians 5:1, says our bodies are like tents that will be destroyed one day and God will give us a place to live after our tents have been destroyed. That clearly means that the Spirit that lives inside me will live forever; right?

Galatians 6:1, tells us that we are a Spirit, which makes 1 Corinthians 3:16, true that God's Spirit lives inside us. Yet John 4:24 tells us the God is a Spirit. So the Spirit that lives in you is God. So it's true that 99% of who we are is the inside of our bodies; the Spirit that lives inside us. Now in the book of Genesis 1:28, God says bring the earth under your control. That means after He had created us and placed us here on earth, He wanted us to control everything on earth since He has given us His powers and tool to control everything on earth. In fact, God is inside you right now as I speak and you are god 1 Corinthians 3:16 say so.

Now let's look at the words God says, "Bring the earth under **your control**". What does He mean by this? Let's look at the word "control". What does control mean? It means to have command and to exercise the power within you. And what does exercise means? It means to make use of your powers and put them into action. So that is what God wanted us to do after He placed us here on earth, to use and put into action the powers inside us in this present moment. God is wise after all, He knew that some people won't understand all of this and so He had to use his own voice, the Word to send the message to everyone so that people could understand Him and His plans.

So in the book of Psalms 82:6 He says "I, The Most High God say that all of you are gods and also my children." The capital G in God stands for The Most High God, the creator of heavens and earth. Then the small g in god stands for the gods of the nations that God defeated. But it also stands for God's servants, human rulers or human beings just like me and you. But throughout this whole book I will be talking about the god which is a human being; me and you; the power that lies within us. And don't get this wrong, you are still god and we also share the same Spirit with The Most High God; which can create everything on earth, as He said in Genesis.

Now God has used His Word to tell us that we are gods, oh yes, I'm talking to you. God has said it Himself that you are god. What did The Most High God mean by this? Let's look at the meaning of the word God. The word God means it's a superhuman being that have powers over nature and controls everything that is around. Now let's take a look at the word superhuman. Superhuman means greater than normal powers. It is the power that lies inside you right now.

So this verse means that we are children of The Most High God who breathed life into us Genesis 2:7. And the time He breathed life into us He was giving us the power and tool to create and control everything here on earth. As He also said it in Genesis 1:28, "bring the earth **under your control**." That's why The Most High God calls us gods, because He knows that He has already given us His power to control everything on earth. He even continued in the book of Exodus 3:14-15 and God said to Moses, I am the eternal God. So tell them that the Lord, whose name is "I AM", has sent you. This is my name for ever, and it is the name that **the people must use** from now onwards.

As God says for ever, it's because this is something that would never change. I am who I am. Now let me ask you something, if you say I AM, who are you referring too? Yes yourself, not me, your neighbour or somebody else. When you say I AM, you are talking about yourself; the real you who lies within.

First God has told you that you are god, and secondly that He is I AM and thirdly that from now onwards you must use "I am" every time because you are god. Do you know how powerful these two words "I AM" are? Oh yes they are powerful especially when they are used together, and let me tell you how.

When you say "I" it's relating to the speaker and he/she is showing the action of a sentence that is done or felt by the subject of the sentence. Then "AM" is used before a present participle to show that the action is taking place as you speak. "AM" is also used to show the future and it's also used to form the passive; and the word passive means the acceptance of the power.

So when you say "I am" you are talking about yourself and the action of what you are saying is taking place as you speak. You also creating the future for yourself and you are accepting the power that is taking place as you are saying "I am". So whenever you use these two words, be careful of what you say after these two words because you are creating the future for yourself.

Remember that you are god and you create everything you say with your voice just like God created heavens and earth using His Voice, The Word. Let's look in the book of John 10:34-35, Jesus replied, "In your scriptures doesn't God say, you are gods? **You cannot argue with the scriptures**."

Now these two verses clearly states that you are god and you cannot argue with the scriptures because it is God's Word. Now I'm sure that most of you if not all would agree that Jesus Christ came into this world to show me and you how we should live here on planet earth.

Jesus also said in John 14:10, don't you believe that I am one with The Father and that The Father is one with me? What I say isn't said on my own. The Father who lives in me does these things. In this verse we hear Jesus using the words "I AM". In the scriptures it tells us that God is I AM and we should also use the words "I am" from now onwards (Exodus 3:14-15).

So Jesus is also telling us that God lives in Him and everything that he says is not said by only him, but the person who is living inside him who is God, the same God that lives in you right now. Now let's look at the trinity. It's true that God the Father + Jesus the Son + the Holy Spirit = One person.

Now John 4:24 tells us that God is a Spirit, then John 14:10 Jesus tells Philip that he is one with The Father and that God The Father lives in Him. That means the Spirit God lives in Jesus. Remember that Jesus Christ was born just like me and you, and he came to this world to show us how to live our lives on a daily bases.

In fact Jesus was telling us that every person on earth that was born just like him has a Spirit inside them, and what you need to do is to activate the Holy Spirit; The God inside you right now by accepting that Jesus came to this world to show us the way to live our lives. So it's also true that God the Father + the Son (including **you**) + the Holy Spirit = One person (John 17:21). That's why we say God is our Father, because we are His children just like Jesus Christ is. Now I hope that everyone will understand the trinity clearly from now onwards.

Ok, let me put it in another way using the scriptures so you could understand the trinity much better. Colossians 2:9-10, "For in him the whole fullness of Deity [the Godhead] continues to dwell **in bodily form** [giving complete expression of the divine nature]. And you are in him, made full and having come to fullness of life [in Christ **you too** are filled with the Godhead- Father, Son, Holy Spirit- and reach full spiritual stature]. And He is the Head of all rulers and authority [of every angelic principality and power]".

1 Corinthians 3:16 tells us that God lives inside us. Galatians 6:1 tells us that we are all Spirits, and that means we are all gods, Psalms 82:6 confirms that. Once you understand this, you'll know that you have the power within you right now as I speak; especially to those who believe.

You will also know that you can create anything and everything with the powers that you have right now. You should start using your powers from today, and now. That's why you'll find some people saying that there are things hidden in the Bible or the Bible is a secret or you need to have some sort of a kind of a Holy Spirit to understand the Bible.

Well, let me tell you that these notions are not true, why? It is because you have the same Holy Spirit that Jesus Christ has within you right now, and the only thing you need to do is activate it so it will work for you. If there is a secret in the Bible, that means I have just revealed everything to you and you know the secret now.

Remember the first words that God our Father said after He created us (Genesis 1:28), bring the earth under **your control**. Now it's time to be aware and start creating and controlling everything on earth with what you have right now. Through these few verses I just wanted to show you with proof from the scriptures that you are god and He lives inside you in this present moment as I speak. You are able to be and do everything you want to do with the help of the information I'm going to share with you as you continue to read.

I once read a book which is selling like hot cakes, and this book is written by a pastor. I'm not a pastor but as much as I agree with him in most of the things he is saying in his book. There is one thing I have noticed that I didn't agree with because the scriptures tell me something else.

The pastor has quoted the Bible verses throughout his book but he didn't quote any verse to support his notion. The pastor said in his book, "You are not god and can never be god." Let me tell you that this notion is incorrect and anyone who tells you that you a not god has not studied The Word of God properly.

I have already quoted from the scriptures where it tells me that I am god and I'm sure that your Bible is also telling you clearly that you are god, Psalms 82:6. It continues to tell us that we cannot argue with the scriptures, John 10:34-35.

If you don't believe that you are god, I challenge you right now to look back into your past life and check if you didn't create your past experiences and your current experience; the situation you are in right now. It's either you created your life by the choices of words you used, or by the beliefs that you had, or it was either by the way you thought.

I'm sure that if you sit back and start to think now and hard about your past, you'll eventually see and know that I'm 100% right. You were creating everything for yourself because you are the creator of your own life and you have always been a creator all this time.

It's just that as you were creating your life you were unconscious and now I have made you conscious on everything you were creating. Let me show you now on how to direct and control your life as you continue to read.

Again, I read a book which I will call it "book X" for now. This book was criticising "The Secret" by Rhonda Byrne one of the bestselling books. Book X was saying that we can never be God or like God. The author of book X even quoted a verse in Jeremiah 10:23 which read as, "I know Lord that we humans are not in control of our own lives." Now as the author of book X has quoted this verse, he is clearly saying that we as human cannot be in control of our lives and we cannot be god or be like God, and therefore the power comes from the outside.

What amazes me is that the author of book X is also quoting from the scriptures but interpreting the verses wrongly. Now let me tell you what Jeremiah meant when he prayed and said, "I know Lord that we humans are not in control of our own lives."

Yes I agree that we cannot do anything by ourselves because we are just tents that we live in, but the Spirit which is God (John 4:24) that lives inside our tents/bodies is the one that makes everything possible. And everyone that worships God must be led by the Spirit that lives in our bodies.

God even said in Jeremiah 31:33 that He will write His Laws in **our** minds and hearts and again in Hebrews 8:10 the same thing is said onto us. Now this is what Jeremiah meant, that our bodies cannot do anything by themselves and God who is the Spirit and lives inside the body can do things and make everything else possible.

This clearly shows that all the power comes from the inside and even when God said in the beginning Genesis

1:28, bring the earth under your control. He said this because He knew that He was going to give us His power when He breathes life into us, and we will be able to do or create anything we desire here on earth.

Hence I have already quoted from the scriptures that God made humans to be like Himself and He also told us that we are gods. Some people and some Christians tend to not believe in the books like "The Secret" because they leave God out of the equation and they believe in the universe.

Let me tell you that these books like "The secret" are in line with the Bible and everything that they talk about you'll find it in the Bible. The only difference is that they leave God and/or Jesus out of the equation and talk about the universe.

I will show you that God is above everything else and God's Spirit wants us to be successful and wealthy. It's all given to us through the Bible. The only difference you'll find is that some people are successful and some are not. This is because God has given us a choice to make. Some people make the right choice and become successful, while others make the wrong choice and they keep on being poorer. It's all up to us to be successful or be poor; the choice is just yours alone.

Don't worry or panic; I will show you step by step throughout this book on how to become successful like you were created to be. I'll take you step by step as a child that just started to walk but cannot walk properly.

A lot of authors in their miracle coaching's and some authors which are included in "The Secret" if not all will tell you that you are god, and I have also shown you that God also said that you are god through the scriptures (Psalms 82:6).

Dr Joe Vitale was also asked in one of the television shows about where God fits in "The secret" and his response was that god is all of us. And he was 100% right. It's also true that I am god, you are god and we are all gods.

John 17:22-23 Jesus prayed to God and said, "They may be one with each other, just as we are one. I am one with them and you are one with me, so that they may become completely one." So now in this verse when Jesus says he is one with us, and The Father is one with him, that clearly states that we are also one with The Father, and we are all combined in one Spirit.

Let's take a look at another verse, John 14:20 Jesus said to his disciples, "You will know that I am one with The Father. You will know that you are one with me, and I am one with you." Again in the book of John 15:4-7 Jesus said to his disciples, "Stay joined to me, and I will stay joined to you. Just as a branch cannot produce fruit unless it stays joined to the vine, you cannot produce fruit unless you stay joined to me."

By this statement Jesus meant that you should always stay connected with the Spirit of God that lives in you so you can be, and do everything you wish to do. He understood that the only thing or person that can make everything possible for you is the inner man.

"I am the vine, and you are the branches. If you stay joined to me, and I stay joined to you, then you will produce lots of fruit. But you cannot do anything without me." I don't know if you still need me to explain this verse as well. But it says everything. It is clear that the Spirit has power and can control everything around us.

"If you don't stay joined to me, you will be like dry branches that are gathered up and burnt in a fire." That's why you'll see people being broke and poor; they are like dry branches which are burnt in a fire; and we tend to feel sorry for them. Do you also want to be like a dry branch which is always in the fire and have no money to satisfy their needs?

I'm sure you wouldn't want that, so now let me show you how to change so you can produce big and fresh fruits. Where you come from is never an issue. We have seen a lot of homeless people become millionaires. So what's stopping you to become a multimillionaire while you still even have a shelter; or you just happy with your current position because you have a shelter?

My friend, you need to change and change now. Connected with the Spirit; the greatness that lies within you right now. This is the Man you should connect with so you can change your life and be in control of everything and everyone around you.

"Stay joined to me and let my teachings become part of you. Then you can pray for **whatever** you want, and your prayer **will be answered**." Yes it's true that Jesus came to teach us everything and how to live on earth. Don't even think that he is the only one who can do what he did.

He did his share in showing us the way and he is in Heaven, now it's you turn to do what he did; and you can even do greater things than he did. Take note that there is no limit in whatever you pray or ask for. "**Pray for whatever you want, and your prayer will be answered.**" He even said it himself in John 14:12, "I tell you for certain that if you have **faith** in me, you will do the same things that I am doing. You will even do greater things, now that I am going back to The Father."

So you tell me, what more can you really ask for? Everything we have already been given and we place little value on the things that are given to us for free, and we end up not using them at all. John 15:7 then continues to say, pray for whatever you want and your prayer will be answered. What are you doing exactly when you pray? You are asking and requesting for whatever you are praying for, and by the amount of faith you have and use, you will receive everything you have prayed for.

Some Christians including the writer of book X, says that Jesus is God, but they don't believe that they themselves are god. Let's go a bit deeper with what I'm saying.

Galatians 4:4-6 says, "But when the time was right, God sent His Son, and a woman gave birth to him. His Son obeyed the Law, so he could set us free from the Law, and we could become God's children. Now in this verse it clearly states that Jesus is God's son. His son came to this world to set us free from the Law of sin and death, so we could become God's children as well.

"Now that we are His children, God has sent the Spirit of His son into our hearts. And his Spirit tells us that God is our Father." And now that we are God's children, He sent the Spirit of His son Jesus into our hearts. Now this verse clearly states that Jesus is God's Son and we are also God's sons because of His Spirit that is within us. Obviously if Jesus is God's son and I'm also God's son, Jesus is my brother and I can do whatever he did because Our Father gave us the same Spirit that Jesus has; just as He promised in Joel 2:28. "Later, I will give my Spirit to everyone. Your sons and daughters will prophesy. Your old men will have dreams, and your young men will see visions".

Hebrews 2:16-17 "Jesus clearly did not come to help angels, but he did come to help Abraham's descendants." That's us, me and you. "He had to be one of us." So if Jesus was like me and you, it shows that everything that he did, you can also do it and even more.

Now let me explain and show you in the scriptures that Jesus said he is god; and that we are all connected. He also **didn't** call himself God, The Most High, but acknowledges God who is The Father, The Creator.

John 5:18 "Now the leaders wanted to kill Jesus for two reasons. First, he had broken the Law of the Sabbath. But even worse, he had said that God was his Father, which made him equal with God"

John 14:9-14 Jesus replies to Philip's comment, "Philip, I have been with you for a long time. Don't you know who I am? If you have seen me, you have seen The Father. How can you ask me to show you The Father?

Don't you believe that I am one with The Father and that The Father is one with me? What I say isn't said on my own. The Father who lives in me does these things. Have faith in me when I say that The Father is one with me and that I am one with The Father. Or else have faith in me simply because of the things I do.

I tell you for certain that if you have faith in me, you will do the same things that I am doing. **You will even do greater things**, now that I am going back to The Father. Ask me, and I will do whatever you ask. This way the son will bring honour to The Father. I will do whatever you ask me to do." With these verses I can clearly tell that there is no limit in praying or asking for what you desire.

Remember that when you are praying, you are actually asking and requesting whatever you are thinking about. The minute you get clear about what you are thinking about, you are asking for it to take place in your life.

Earl Nightingale once said, "We become what we think about." Obviously this statement is true because the Bible tells us that when you pray for something, you will receive what you have asked for.

Wayne Dyer was also correct when he said, "You have the power within you to attract to yourself all that you could ever want." The Bible also confirms this statement with what Jesus said in John 14:14 and 15:7. "Pray for **whatever** you want and your prayer will be answered."

Let's take a look at another verse which tells us about God. Matthew 28:6, Jesus told his disciples that they must baptise the people in the name of The Father, The Son and The Holy Spirit. Take note that he didn't say baptise the people in the name of The Father, myself and The Holy Spirit.

Why is that so? It's because Jesus knew that when a person is being baptise, they are doing it for themselves and not someone else. The Father stands for The Most High God, the Son stands for your body, the tent that you live in since you are the Son of The Father, and the Holy Spirit stands for the person that lives inside you, who is God, The Creator of everything, and John 4:24 confirms this statement.

I totally agree with Marianne Williamson when she said, **"At our core, we are not just identical, but actually the same being as Christ."** But the author of the book X doesn't agree with this statement. I have already shown you that the Bible says that and I agree with it all the way. Bob Proctor once said, **"I'm not a body, but I live in a body"**. This is true, you are not a body, but you live in a body and all the power comes from within your body; the real you who is the Spirit.

Chapter 2
THE MIND POWER

The way the minds of some people operate is such a shocking matter. It's a very serious issue and it's not funny at all. People will forget special days like the human rights day and recognise this day like one of the holiday that was given to them so they could drink alcohol when they are not working or not at school; yet they will make sure they remember a day like April fools. These types of people will make sure that the first thing they will do in the morning on the 1st of April is to make as many people seem like fools.

They will plan and come up with a huge story so that everyone will believe it whenever they deliver the message. This person will be so happy to see the person who he/she told lies too getting worried and panicking. Forgetting that this day won't add value to his/her life, but it puts a risk in somebody's life. We have heard stories of some people committing suicide because of these unnecessary jokes that have been made on this day.

The way these people have programmed their minds is to make other people fools, and most importantly they make themselves fools as well, but they unaware of that. These people will sit for hours planning a huge story for the 1st of April and not realising the damage they are doing to their minds. They sit and think about useless and unworthy things, and they are just programming the mind to think only about useless and unworthy things.

They are creating their minds to be useless tools which draw unneeded and unwanted things into their lives. Later on a person will wonder why there is no growth in his/her life. This is the trick about the mind; everything you joke about or say will become your reality. The mind will make you believe these things and as much as you're saying them to the next person, they come back directly to you.

I'm here to show you how to eliminate all the unwanted things and draw only success into your life. Just as you direct your hand using your mind to touch or pick up anything, it's the same way of how to direct your mind in getting all the success that you need into your life.

Every day comes with hundreds, thousands and even millions of opportunities that have never been discovered before. If only you could find one opportunity from the millions that have never been discovered, do you understand how successful and wealthy will you be?

If we look back 100 years from now, can we see ourselves living in that time? I'm sure your answer will be no, then my next question will be why? I think it's clear that the world was not developed enough just like the way it is today. I believe you would find it very difficult to live back in the 100 years clearly because you already used to the technology that we have today.

But did the people who lived in 1915 find the world in that state they lived in? The answer is no, but it took real people who are just like me and you to sit down and think hard about what they want to achieve in life.

Now if you look from 1915 till now, can you see how everything has changed and how technology has moved from one point to another? 28 years ago when I was born, they were no cell phones but today we have different kinds of cell phones. Who even thought that a cell phone would talk or read an incoming message to you?

At the time I was born, I remember that at home we had a television box that was made out of wood. But if you look in today's televisions we have LCD's and plasma's. Who thought that back in the days we would have televisions or plasmas that we have today?

I also remember that at home we also had a vinyl player that was also made out of wood. At that time I have never even seen a disc or a disc player, but today we don't even have discs only, we now have USBs. I can go on and on about the technology and the changing of everything in the world. But my point is; do you really see how technology is changing each day?

Now how did everything become like this today if you compare it back in 100 years from now? The answer is simple, it took some people to use their minds and think;

people who were born like me and you; people who have the same mind-set like me and you; people who decided to use their minds, not sit on it.

Nothing exists by itself, but it took people to use their minds and think. Just by you thinking and inventing what they have thought about, made those people very rich. What did really make these people rich? It's the same mind-set that you have currently with right now.

The only difference they made is just to think a bit more than the average people. Most people don't really use their minds nor should I say they use their minds on useless things, things that won't help them in future.

Now if you look into the future from now on to the next 100 years, can you picture how would the world look? Everything will be changed, maybe the cell phones will be much smaller, maybe a new communicating system; are better and advanced plasmas and I believe that the people who will be living in those times won't be even using USBs, but something far better than that. But it will take people who will use their minds to think and make a change in this world.

Everything starts within your mind. Just think about it for a minute; if you are one of those people who are going to make a change in the next 100 years from now; can you imagine how rich you would be? Can you think about your kids, your grandchildren and your whole family that will still come to this world how rich they will be just because of you?

I'm not saying that you must only think about inventing something, but what I'm saying here is that you need to think, so that you can make your life better. No one can think for you except for yourself. You are the only one who is doing the thinking part in your mind, and you also the only one who can control and guide your mind on what to think about.

Just by improving yourself and your life; can you imagine how many people you will be helping starting by your own family? For example, your kids in better schools, eating what you love in whatever time you wish to eat, living in your dream house and driving one of the best cars in the whole world. But all of this has to start within you right now and change the way you do things, and also change the way you think. If you want to change your current lifestyle, start by changing the way you think.

In Jeremiah 31:33 and again in Hebrews 8:10 God said that He will write His Laws in your mind. What does He mean by this? He means that He is going to give you the ability to use your mind and think with it; to know what's right or wrong without even waiting for someone to tell you. It also mean that no one else can jump into your head and think for you; you are the only person who can do the thinking for yourself, and if you don't think, you will be stuck since you cannot even hire someone to think for you.

Proverbs 15:26 God hates unpleasant and harmful thoughts. It's like this, every thought that you think about, you're creating for it to take place. Whether those harmful thoughts are about yourself or somebody, they will come looking for you.

When your thoughts are harmful to other people, don't think that you are also safe because what you have done is; you have created a path of harmful things to come looking for you and to come your way. Let me tell you how this is possible. In Genesis 2:7 God breathed life into a man and we are all connected through His breath that He gave Adam. And again we all come from Adam and Eve which makes us to be all connected and one.

That is why you don't necessarily need to think about harmful thoughts about yourself for them to take place. Just by you thinking of them even when you direct them to someone else, they come indirectly back to you. And that is why it is important to think about pleasing thoughts only, at all times; because by doing that you'll be helping yourself and creating a path of pleasing things to flow into your life.

When you think about unpleasant and harmful thoughts like in Psalms 56:5, you are not only creating harmful things to come looking for you, but you are also wasting your precious time that can never be replaced. If only you invest that time in yourself and think about clear and pure thoughts only like it says in Psalms 51:10, you'll be helping yourself and bringing success closer and faster to yourself.

You know, people are so funny. They would prefer to invest outside the mind with the hairstyles that they do weekly, more than to invest in the inside of their minds with the books that they read. Nowadays people don't even care on what's going on inside their minds, and not only that, they underestimate the power of the mind. People tend to place little value to the things that are given to them for free, which they didn't pay anything for. Your mind is one of them and a very powerful tool you'll ever have in your whole life.

If you're one of these people who don't appreciate the mind and doesn't understand that the mind is one of the tools that create your future, you need to change and come to realise that everything is done with the mind. The fact that you have the mind; it shows that you can also be a very rich person from today.

2 Corinthians 5:13 informs us that when you feel like you're losing your mind, it's between you and your God. You need to connect with Him so you can regain your life and be in control at all times. And if you are in your perfect set of mind and connecting with your God like you should be, it is for your own good and no one else. You'll also be glad that you positioned your mind in a perfect state since you create everything with it.

Ecclesiastes 5:2 warns you that you should think first before you speak. Again this verse shows you that your mind is powerful and controls everything; and if you don't use your mind to think first, everything else will go wrong. Ecclesiastes 5:3 tells you that your mind is in control and if you continue to think about the same thing, you will dream about it and it will take place in your life.

Bear in mind that when you are dreaming about something you are inventing and creating what you thinking about to become a reality whether it's good or bad. You also hoping and expecting your dream to come true; and you are basically putting everything to work and in a process to achieve what you are thinking or dreaming about.

Fools will think of foolish things and create negative things to flow into their lives, but wise people will think and dream about good things and they will allow positive things which will work in favour for them to flow into their lives.

Philippians 4:7, when you obey God's Laws, He will bless you with inner peace which will help you to control the way you think, talk and feel. You need to start controlling your mind so you can be in control of your life. If you let your mind wonder around without any direction, your life too will wonder around without any direction. Be in control to achieve all your desires.

Philippians 4:8 make sure that you always think about what is pure and proper at all times and make sure you don't ever stop thinking about what you want to achieve. Make it your habit that you think about it all the time, day and night.

Live in your mind and see your dream happening and what you thinking about turn into a reality. This is the most powerful way to make your dreams and goals come to you as fast as possible. If you spend less time thinking about your dreams, it will take longer to accomplish them, and if you think about them every time, they will come to you faster.

Live in your mind and dwell on what you want to be, and everything else will grow into its place like you have asked for it to happen. **Do not** dwell on negative things even if that is your current situation because you're recreating them to keep on taking part in your life.

Change your current situation by the way you think and dwell on what you want to see it happen so it will become your reality. Everything is done with and by the mind. Nothing comes to life without the mind; you are the creator and you need to start controlling your thoughts.

Remember that you become what you think about; and this is so true. Now as a creator with your mind creating your future, everything that you think of today, if it won't help you in future, you need to realise and release that now, and change the way you think. The past can never be changed, but your future can be changed by the way you think from now onwards.

You only need to believe on what you're thinking about to turn what's in your mind into a reality. Use your mind at all times to get what you desire. Use what you have to obtain what you want. You must know that the negative thoughts will still come into your mind, but you'll need to ignore them and don't concentrate on them, but put all your focus to the positive thoughts you want to turn into a reality. What you need to do is to control and train your mind to do what you want it to think and concentrate on that, and in that way you'll be helping yourself.

You know, all around the world people always disagree about something and never get to agree with each other, but there's this one thing they have agreed upon. They all agree that everything starts in the mind, and I happen to agree with them 100%, don't you?

If you also agree with this statement, so why do you place little value on your mind and your ability to think? Why do you underrate and underestimate the power of your mind? If you really know and hear people say that everything starts in the mind, so why don't you use it and start to create a better future for yourself?

Everything has to start from within, and success has to grow from the inside to the outside. The power lies in you and not on someone else. Everyone is responsible for their own success, and when are you planning to be in control of your own success?

You must know that your mind works like a bank, and whatever you deposit in it will be received back with interest. The more you deposit, the more you will receive; and whatever you deposit, you will receive exactly what you deposited in return. It as simple as that and it will always work like that.

2 Timothy 3:8-9, tell us that when your mind and faith is not strong and you suffering; you won't get far in life. 1 Corinthians 2:11, you are the only one who knows what's in your mind, and therefore you are the only person who can control everything in your mind.

Now since you know that the mind is the creator of everything and if you don't direct your mind to what you want to achieve, you won't get anywhere in life because no one can jump into your mind and control it for you to the direction you want to pursue.

Proverbs 4:23 tells us to carefully guard our thoughts because they are the only **true source** of life. Your thoughts are the only thing that will create your future, and if you control and direct them to what you desire, the outcome will be exactly what you thought about.

Now let me tell you a short story about what happened to me. After being in a car accident in 2010 and the car I was driving was beyond repairs; I told myself that I will never be in an accident or smash a car I would be driving again.

All the past years I have been in so many car accidents, in fact every three months I smashed a car I was driving while I was drunk. But after telling myself that I would never smash a car again, that's what really happened, I never did.

I would be drunk and have a few long blackouts while driving, and I wouldn't even know on how I got home safely. But since I told myself and recorded that in my mind that I would never smash a car again, my words were fulfilled. I stopped smashing cars and till today I have never been in a car accident and by faith in God I won't ever be in a car accident again. I have told myself that and I have recorded that deep in my mind.

Now through this testimony from the many that I have; I have come to realise that everything you need is inside of you right now as I speak. You can heal and direct your life with just your thoughts. The only thing you have to do is just to think and already you're building your tomorrow.

Think of the person inside of you, the inner man as a form of water. Whatever you think or plan whether good or bad, it will take place. If you dig a whole and pour water inside, the water will go inside and stay there because there is no way that it wouldn't go in.

Just like the person who is inside you right now, the inner man, who is the true you and lives within your body, he will help you to achieve everything that's on your mind. Think it and you'll achieve it.

Chapter 3
THE WORD

I'm sure most people will agree with me that the Bible is a book of encouragement. And again I'm sure most people if not all will agree with me that Jesus came to this world to show us the way to live life, just like it should be; through faith.

I have also shown you in chapter one through the scriptures that Jesus is our brother and we are one with him, and also one with The Father. Since Jesus came to show us the way to life, that means you too should walk in his footsteps.

Therefore in some places instead of Jesus you need to put yourself in his shoes so you could understand clearly what he came to teach me and you. In the book of John 14:12, Jesus said, "I tell you for certain that if you have faith in me, you will do the same things that I am doing. You will even do greater things, now that I am going back to The Father."

Since Jesus is on the right hand side of The Father (Ephesians 1:20), we should take his place here on earth, and heed to his commission. He is also informing us that we can do the same things that he did and also do even greater things if only we have **faith**. "For in him the whole fullness of Deity [the Godhead] continues to dwell **in bodily form** [giving complete expression of the divine nature]. And you are in him, made full and having come to fullness of life [in Christ **you too** are filled with the Godhead- Father, Son, Holy Spirit- and reach full spiritual stature]. And He is the Head of all rule and authority [of every angelic principality and power]" (Colossians 2:9-10).

I need you to understand these basics so you can understand how powerful you are and where does all this power comes from. To make it worse, Jesus was here on earth to show and teach us how does the power we possess works. But still people enjoy keeping their eyes closed and they really don't want to open their spiritual eyes to the truth.

John 1:1-3 "In the beginning was the one who is called The Word. The Word was with God and was truly God." Please take note that the Spirit that lives inside you was long alive before you were even born. We all belong to one Spirit that was long alive before we were stored in a bodily form. Rewind to the time you were born. In the beginning was the one who is called The Word.

Now who is The Word? The Word is in **you.** He lives in you and He is the one who speaks through you. The Word of God uses **your voice** when He speaks. The Word was with God and was truly God. Remember that

God is a Spirit and that Spirit lives in you, as shown in chapter one.

"From the very beginning The Word was with God. And with this Word, God created all things. Nothing was made without The Word." And with The Word, which is God, God created everything. Nothing was made without The Word.

This is plain and simple to understand and it comes as a surprise to some people. Now I have revealed the mystery of God. Once you understand the power in your voice and that you create everything with it. You would have mastered the basics, and that is why it is vital to control every word that will come out from your month.

If you look back into your life, you will see that you also created your current situation with the words you spoke. And from now onwards you'll take note of the words you use and see where they will lead you in future.

I'm saying all this because of my experience as well. My entire life journey was created by the choice of words I used. As I am in prison, I created everything with what I said, and what I had said became a reality 10 days later after I had said it.

Psalms 141:3 is a prayer to the Lord in asking Him for protection to guard your words every time you speak. But you still don't listen and choose to ignore this verse. That is why you have crisis in the world around you; it's because of the choice of words you used before, which created everything around you, just like I did.

Again Proverbs 18:20-21 tell us that we should speak good words because later you'll be happy that you did. All the words that you speak today can bring death or life tomorrow. Everything you speak today will happen onto you. This is exactly what happened with my life. Everything I had said before became a reality and I had to live and swim in everything that I had said before.

Proverbs 15:2, a wise person will always speak wisdom, and a fool will just speak anyhow and fail to control his/her words. Proverbs 15:4 tell us that if we speak good words, they will be like medicine, but a bad choice of words will hurt you and even a doctor can't help you if you hurt in the inside. Doctors only help people in the things that can be seen, but with the things that cannot be seen, you are the only one who can help yourself. A good choice of words at the right time will heal, and it's like the finest gold on earth, Proverbs 25:11.

If you want to go somewhere in life and be successful, focus on the good things and the positive ones and speak life into them. And that is when you'll see a huge change in your life. If you gossip about other people, you won't become a better person. All the attention, time and energy are going to the people you are talking about, as well as the things that won't help you to achieve what you desire in your life.

Stop gossiping and all the other unnecessary things you talk about, and let the good things flow into your life. People who are constructively involved with their own lives have little time to interfere with the lives of the other people.

Eliphaz, Job's friend was telling Job that the way he was so influential to other people his words could lead everyone to have doubts about God, with the deceitful mind as the source of everything he says (Job 15:4-5). Job's friends were attacking him with painful words without any reason to do so. They inflicted more pain with the choice of words they used. Eliphaz also touched a very important issue when he said the mind is a **source of everything** that you say. The mind and your words work hand in hand and cannot be separated. The mind thinks about what it is going to say, and the mouth utters those words.

Foolish talks will burn, ruin and bring you down to your knees and you will eat everything you have ever said. The words which are spoken by a wise man are the source of true life, and evil people will always speak hurtful words (Proverbs 10:10-11).

The Bible is here to guide us so we can walk through the right and correct path, and that is why we are being informed about these things. The choice is yours after all, to choose between life and death, but God advices us to choose life.

The words of a good person are everything, but the thoughts of an evil person is a waste of energy and good for nothing (Proverbs 10:20). Like I said, the mind and your tongue work hand in hand. They are like business partners which can never be separated.

Your mind is the boss or the main partner, and your voice takes instructions from the mind. Everything the mind instructs to be done, your voice follow the command that has already been given by the mind. Everything and I mean everything you say is the outcome of what you have been feeding your mind throughout the years. The production takes place in the mind and your mouth produces what have been manufactured in your brain.

Let me give you an example of one of the powers that the voice has. A Judge in a court room will sentence someone to prison for a certain period of time and that person serves that particular time that was said by the voice. The word the judge speaks is put into action and a lot of people will follow those words.

The person who is sentenced has no choice but to follow as instructed, and also the prison warders will also follow what was said in court. Even though they were not in court or even heard those words being spoken, but they will believe what was said and written down.

Now my question to you is; can we freely speak our minds at any time without fear of suffering the consequences at a later stage? I'm sure you have the answer by now. The answer is no. If you speak freely and anyhow, you will reap what you sow and you will eat everything you have ever said. And it's too bad that you can't even take the words back after you have said them.

Do not speak without thinking (Ecclesiastes 5:2). As I have said before, you are given the free will to speak anything you wish to speak, but you are given advice on what to do. Thinking before you speak will always help you. And following this example has also made me to come back on track.

Every single one of us sometimes do unlawful deeds, but as soon as you can control your tongue, you are fully grown and that means you can control your entire body. If you want to control a horse, you need to put a bit into the mouth of the horse in order for you to control it.

Same applies when the captain wants to control a ship. He uses a small helm to direct the ship to pursue his destination. Now these two points I have mentioned are a good example of our tongues. The tongue is very small but it talks about big things. The tongue is a fire that can burn a person's entire life with the amount of fire it possesses.

Every kind of animal is tamed, but the tongue cannot be tamed, it gets out of control and it is evil and full of deadly poison. With the same tongue you possess, you bless and curse people who were created to be like God (James 3:2-10).

Don't let corrupt words proceed out of your mouth, but speak life into people's lives. By doing so, you are helping them and as well as yourself (Ephesians 4:29). Don't use disgusting, dirty, foolish, filthy and indecent words, because all that disgusting dirt will come hunting you back (Ephesians 5:4). Now that is not what you want and need in your life, you only need success and you should eliminate words and things which are going to pull you back.

The law of attraction says, like attracts like. You give out food to the needy and you will attract more food coming into your life. You give out money, and more money will come flowing into your life. Same applies when you are talking. The same things you are saying to or about someone are the same things that will come back flowing into your life. What you give out is exactly what you'll get back.

Talk about negative things about somebody else, negative things will come looking for you. Talk about positive things, and positive things will come looking for you. Tell me, have you ever seen a person who is always gossiping bad things about other people being successful?

I'm sure your answer will be a no, and you are smiling about it because everything I'm telling you adds up now. And you also smiling or laughing because you already have someone you picture in your mind right now, who is always gossiping about other people and his/her life has always been the same with no progress.

Now you should stop wondering why someone who is always gossiping is not moving forward in life, you know the answer to that now. If you are one of those people who are gossipers, you need to make a decision now and change your corrupt talking. What you are doing is only killing you. Remember, the law of attraction says, like attracts like. Even the Bible tells us that you reap what you sow.

Why do you think throughout the book of Proverbs it talks about wisdom? We are told that wise people will speak wise words, and fools will speak foolish words. We are told over and over again about the choices of the words we must use, why is that so? It's very clear that whatever you say, will come looking for you; like attracts like. Talk life into your own life and don't criticise yourself, and then speak life into people's lives and don't criticise anyone. Get this in your head, practice it, and make it your habit and every good thing will start flowing into your own life, simple as that. You need to start realising things now so you can claim what's yours, something that belongs to you. Control your tongue so you can control everything else in your life. The Lord hates evil thoughts because they produce what you will say next. But good thoughts will produce good words and they will please the Lord God (Proverbs 15:26).

You must know that your tongue reflects on your Spirit. It reveals what's inside your heart (Matthew 12:34). Everything that you say with your tongue will tell everyone how your inner man is, and what you have been eating all these years. You only take out what was put in. You just cannot take out what you didn't put in and what you don't have. Everything takes place in the inside and what you say will show what's inside of you. Your tongue only recycles the input of what's already inside you that was put by you and the people around you over the years. Whatever you put in now, it will show tomorrow. You are a product of your past life.

A tongue which loses balance and control is just an obstacle which reflects spiritual immaturity. We cannot be spiritually mature, until we stop using offensive words or remarks against other people. Ecclesiastes 5:6 warns us to not allow our tongues to put us in a huge mess and remember that what have been said cannot be taken back.

Don't say something that will make God angry because He will take everything that you have ever worked for. This goes back to you controlling your tongue. If you control your tongue always and speak life into everything and everyone, God will be happy and bless you with more things you desire into your life. Your words should be a lamp that produces light everywhere you go (Psalms 119:105) and by this you will be honouring God.

With the power of the tongue/voice, I have seen some prisoners controlling life even on the outside world while they are in prison. These prisoners run businesses while they inside the prison and they do all this with the power of the tongue.

They use the telephones to speak with the people on the outside world and they don't even need to see the person to make sure that the business is running well. I'm talking about prisoners who have been incarcerated for years, yet they still make money and feed their families while they are in prison. These prisoners are prisoners who refused to live by hand outs and they will tell you that when a chance presents itself, you must grab it and use it to your fullest ability.

The power of the mind and tongue is exercised and it shows how powerful these two things are when they work together. Yet, you'll find people who are not in prison fail to support themselves. While I'm in prison, I normally say that some people are just better off inside the prison walls because these people are free on the outside world but they are wasting time and doing nothing with their lives while they still have a chance. They are free and nothing is holding them back, but they choose to live by hand outs.

I also used everything that I am explaining in this book and I spoke positive words into my life and the people around me. And it all started in the **inside** of the prison walls. This is another way of showing you that everything starts from the inside and it's easier to control your life on the outside because the hard work has already been done on the inside. I wrote this book while I am in prison; writing it in private, and now I'm rewarded in public for the work I did on the inside.

It's never too late; you too can start to change and direct your life to the place you want to be in, and it will all depend on the decision you take from now onwards.

Let's take another look at the power of the tongue/voice; the radio, presenters and listens. I'm one of the many people who enjoy listening to radio more than watching television. I connect more with the people I'm listening to more than the ones I could be watching on television.

People kiss and make up on radio while they don't even see each other, and it goes back to the power of the tongue. Some people are married today while they found love through radio, cell phones and the internet. Everything on radio is done by the voice. It's overwhelming when sometimes I hear someone donating food to a disadvantaged listener without even meeting the person.

All of this is done through the radio and it's done with the power of the tongue. It's doesn't mean that you need to see the person personally to support him/her. Everything is created and done by the mind and the tongue proceeds and produces what has already been created by the mind. The voice can heal lives, and you too can start healing people and yourself with your own voice. The inner man makes everything possible for you if only you believe.

Matthew 12:37, there will be a time where you will face trail and be informed about the things you have spoken, whether you'll be guilty or innocent everything lies within you. There are absolutely no words that you speak that will go without being answered and that's why it's very vital to guard your tongue.

Everything is said in the Bible but people choose not to notice all these things or they just ignore it. Then whenever you eat what you have said over the past days, it will be like God is unfair to you even though you praise Him day and night.

Let me tell you that if you don't guard you thoughts and tongue, you will eat everything that you think and talk about and it would be like God has left you. Yet you are the one who left God through the things you think and talk about. Remember that you are the creator of your own life and whatever you think and talk about will take place and become a reality.

1 John 1:1 says that, "The Word that gives life was from the beginning and this is the one our message is all about. Our ears have heard, our own eyes have seen, and our hands touched this Word." I have already explained who The Word is; and this verse informs us that your voice gives life.

Our own ears have heard it speaking, our own eyes have seen it, and our own hands have touched this Word. Now I'm sure you must be asking yourself how it's possible now to see and touch the Word, your voice. But from today you should know that everything you see around you right now was created by The Word, someone's voice.

It's either the book you are holding, the cell phone you using or the laptop you are using; everything was created by The Word. People speak their minds out and it's either through the voice or on paper by something that is written or put in pictures.

Nothing is created without the voice, and John 1:3 is telling you that. Even in Genesis 1, in the beginning, everything was being created by the voice, and it's just everything. Now do you understand the power of The Word, **your own** voice?

Do you understand how powerful you are? If you still don't understand the power that lies within you right now, don't worry. I will present more examples for you and you'll just have to prove them yourself so you will be **100%** sure that, everything I say on this book will work. And when you do everything I have told you to do, everything will work for you. Therefore life will work with you to become whatever you desire to be.

We have heard of many incidents when a teenager commits suicide because of what his/her peers were saying. These teenagers say cruel and hurtful words to someone till that kid decides to kill himself/herself. It's either they were informing the deceased about something that is truthful or it was just false information, but at the end of the day someone has died.

What really killed this child? Was it a gun or knife? No, it's only the power of The Word. The things that were said to this teenager eventually killed him/her. You don't even need to see a person or be there to have the power of your voice effective.

You can say something while you are in another country and your orders will be followed. You can say something today and it can take place tomorrow. But what's already been said has to take place and there is no way you can take it back. That is why it is vital to guard everything that you say.

The power of the Word has controlled the world for many years. Today still the Word is controlling the world and it will still control it forever.

Isaiah 42:9 tells us that everything will take place just as you spoke and used your voice. But now since you have a conscious mind with the information I'm presenting to you, it will work in your favour that the next words you say from now onwards will create beautiful things for yourself.

If you believe that you are a child of God but failing to take control your tongue, you are only fooling yourself and you are not a child of God (James 1:26). Everyone who is religious must be able to control everything that comes out from their mouth.

Judges 16:30 tells that Samson created his death with the power of his voice and there was no waiting period because what he said with a strong feeling takes place same time. This is just another way of showing you that your voice has the power to control everything around you.

Another man which created his death with his own voice was Joab. He told Benaiah to kill him at the altar and King Solomon said to Benaiah, do as he said (1 Kings 2:30-31). Then he was killed right there. Joab's God had made what he said and wished for, come into reality.

So again my dear family, I ask you to watch what you say at all times. I am calling you my family because you are really my family. You are my brothers and sisters and by writing this book, it was one of the ways I am showing love to you. So please use my advice or should I say the advice the Bible tells us to use.

1 Samuel 3:19, God fulfilled what was spoken by Samuel and not even one of his words went to waste. It's the same thing I'm trying to express in this book so you could realise your own power that lies within. When you work with your God, He will make sure that every word you speak will come true and be turned in a reality.

Don't say cruel words to anybody because those same words will come looking for you. Say words that are kind and honour everybody so those same words will come looking for you too (Titus 3:2).

Psalms 5:9-10, what you say can destroy you. And if you say wicked and use flatter words against people, God will punish you because of what you have said to your own life. When you plan and say something bad to somebody else, you are saying that same thing onto your own life.

Every word you speak must be a righteous word and not misleading words (Proverbs 8:8). By doing this you are only helping yourself and you will not regret anything in your life if you continue this way. Control your tongue so you'll control your life.

We have been told throughout the Old Testament when God got angry with the people of Israel when they doubted Him and His powers, He punished them. Moses was one of the people who made God very angry and God never allowed him to go through to the Promised Land.

Again we have been shown by Aaron's two sons when they were burnt as a punishment, on what God is capable of doing when He is angry. I was also prosecuted and taken to prison because of my anger. This happened because I failed to control my tongue and feelings.

The emotions that you have are so powerful in a way that they can control anything and anyhow if you don't start to control them yourself. What you think and say with a strong feeling will take place in the fastest speed you can ever imagine. And that is why it is very important to control your feelings, your mind and your tongue.

Now in the book of Jeremiah 31:33 and again in Hebrews 8:10 God said I will make a new covenant for my people. I will write my Laws in their hearts. Now what does that mean? It means that everything that is wrong or right you will know if it's right or wrong before you even do something.

He continued to say I will be their God and they will be my people. Why did He say this? It's because He knows that He lives inside your body right now through His Spirit, and that's why we are able to know if we are doing the right or wrong things at all times.

Have you noticed that whenever you try to do something, there is always that little voice which speaks from the inside of you? It tells you not to do what you are planning to do or it will tell you to do what you have decided to do.

It is always there and it's speaking to you directly. Try and notice it every time you do something, because that is God who is speaking to you. When He says do something, follow those instructions, and when He tells you not to do what you are planning to do, follow those instructions as well.

He lives in you and He cannot leave you. When you work together with Him you allow everything you desire to flow into your life. The Word that speaks to you might be recognised as small, but it isn't. The weight it carries and the ability to do things is just so amazing. God also knew that as we belong to Him, our hearts, emotions will create our future and that is why it is important to control and pay close attention to the way you feel at all times. Numbers 16:46 and again in Numbers 25:4, it is shown that when God is angry, people get killed with our emotions and that's why controlling your temper is important.

The truth to life is within us and in our hearts (2 John 2), and therefore you must pay close attention to what God is saying to you and serve Him according to the truth that is within your heart (1 Samuel 12:24). God is the only person who can make your heart satisfied with bringing all your desires to you, but only if you work together with Him and putting Him in control at all times (Psalms 33:21).

Make sure that you serve the Lord your God with all your heart (Psalms 34:1-2). Your feelings are one of the powerful tools you have to help you equip anything you wish to have. God will bless you with everything you need if you have a good and clean heart (Psalms 73:1)

Tell God that you will always serve Him and worship Him at all times (Psalms 138:1). He is right inside you. Speaking to Him, having a conversation and praying to Him will assist you in being successful and wealthy in the fastest time ever.

Don't worry on how it will happen, but focus on what you say to your God and how you feel. Connect with God, the greatness that lies within you, so He will provide you with peace that will allow you to control the way you feel (Philippians 4:7).

Chapter 4
HOW TO BECOME SUCCESSFUL IN EVERYTHING THAT YOU DO

I will bless you with peace and a future that is bright. A future that will make you very successful and you will not suffer (Jeremiah 29:11). Don't be shaken by the challenges that you a facing today. God has a purpose with your life and He just want to make you strong so that when you arrive and see your purpose in life, you won't be taken down or wiped out by anything or anybody. You will be strong and powerful forever just like Joseph. God allowed the king to send him to prison because God had a purpose for him, and going to prison was part of his journey to his success. Going to prison was not really a problem, but it was a challenge. When the challenge was presented to Joseph, a promotion was also presented to him.

Genesis 39:3 and 39:23 tells us that Joseph became successful in everything that he did. He used his gift that God gave him while he was still inside prison and he became successful in everything that he did. Do you think if Joseph didn't go to prison he was going to be successful like he was? I personally don't think he was going to be successful like he was.

He had to go through the challenge he was faced with first and overcome it so he could be taken to the next stage in life. He had to start somewhere in order for him to get to the next stage of his life. It is true that everything starts from the inside to the outside. Everything starts within your mind to the outside so everybody could see. I'm sure that the same thing happened with Joseph, but let's take a look at another prospective on how Joseph's life was channelled.

Joseph was successful from the inside of the prison and the prison officials didn't worry about anything because they trusted Joseph with everything. Since he was successful inside the prison walls, he also became more successful when he was outside the prison.

It was easy for Joseph to be successful when he was outside the prison because he had already been successful from the inside. When Joseph came out from prison, Potiphar, the official in charge of the palace guard, made Joseph their servant in charge of everything that was in Egypt, and Joseph became more successful and he helped his family and the people of Israel to overcome famine.

This is another method which shows you that everything starts from within. Wherever you are right now and no matter which challenge is facing you currently, you can overcome it with a positive attitude. Don't complain about it, but have faith that it will soon be a great promotion that presented itself and opened room for growth within you.

When I tell you that everything starts from within to the outside, I also understand that what I'm telling you is the only truth. Even Paul wrote his letters that we read about in the Bible while he was still inside the prison. I also wrote this book you are reading now while I am still in prison.

I didn't have to wait to go outside first in order for me to start writing this book. I knew and understood that everything starts from within and I had to take action by starting now. Waiting for tomorrow will never help you; you need to start now so that tomorrow you'll find it easier to continue from where you left off. Immediately when ideas of writing this book came to mind, I just knew that I had to start now and I couldn't wait for the following day.

If you're serious about doing something and you want to be successful, take the action now. Not later today or tomorrow or next week, but do it now. No matter where you are, you can do it at this present moment. If Paul did it while he was still in prison what could stop you? If I also did it while I am still in prison what could stop you now?

If you want to have a business, you must first think about it, than write your plan down and move forward from there. But before a business is brought into a reality, it first had to start in the mind, than on the paper, after that into action.

Again if you want to be fit and grow your muscles, you have to think about it first and see the end result before you even start. Everything is within your mind. Nobody can get inside your head and think for you. You are the only person who can think for yourself and if you don't do it yourself, nobody else can do it for you. It starts in the mind and you must be mentally fit so you can finish what you want to start.

But make sure that every time you want to start doing something, you must first see the end result before you even start doing it. This is one of the main things you should consider before you have to do something; see the end result of it first before you even start your project. Just by thinking it, you are creating it in your mind.

The law of gravity tells us that if you jump from a building you will go down and you can never go up. Same thing applies when you use this book correctly; failure is not even an option, but abundance of success and wealth which will come looking for you. It won't even stop there, but success and wealth will find you and it will stay with you forever. And to make sure that you keep everyone in your family successful and wealthy you just have to teach them everything that is within this book, and I can assure you that even when you long gone from this world, happiness and wealth will always be among your family forever.

Be grateful for waking up, be grateful for the legs you have, be grateful for the hands you have. Be grateful because you still have your body parts. Some people don't have them, but still they make it in life. These kinds of people are not lazy and they strive to better their lives every time. I respect the people with no eyes, hands or legs who are doing something about their lives because they don't just sit around and expect hand outs from the government. Yet you'll find someone who has every part of the body expecting hand outs from the government, and all the other government privileges instead of themselves doing something about their own lives.

Getting a house won't change your life, but it will only provide you with a shelter. And then where will you get food and all the other things you need to survive as a person; plus your family expects you to provide for them? I'm not here to point fingers to some people, but I'm here to tell you that you need to get up and do something about your life. You need to change the way you thinking, and if you start today, I'm sure in the next couple of months you won't be in the same situation as you are in right now. I'm telling you all this because I have been through worse things and the time I told myself that I need to get up and do something about my life, it really happened and my life changed. Everything is possible, and if I did it, you too can also do it. In this way we can all put an end to poverty and a whole lots of other things. If everyone in the world played their part in changing their own life, the world would be a better place and there won't be poverty, or even a word called poverty.

I remember reading an article about a young man who is around the same age as mine, who was graduating and receiving his diploma. This young man was on a wheel chair and he had no legs and he also had no hands. Now do you understand why do I respect people like these?

These are the same people we think we are better than them. The truth must be said that they are the ones who are better than us, because they have achieved what was in their dreams. Then I'll ask myself, what's stopping us to achieve what we want while we still have every part of our bodies?

The answer is simple; **we are too lazy to do anything about our own lives**. We expect hand outs and we are also expecting people to jump into our minds and think for us. I'm telling you my friend that it will never happen. No one will ever be able to think for you, unless you do it yourself.

I can't understand why are we lazy to use our own minds, while we know that we cannot even hire someone to do the thinking for us. You need to start doing something about your own life; get up, do the thinking and make a difference.

Yet again you'll find someone who is blind making means to read something using his fingers. This person will get a clear understand just like you and me. The only different is that he used his hands to read something and you used your eyes.

But at the end we all read something and we all understood what the message was and what was said throughout what we were reading. This clearly shows that there are a lot of ways to get to the same answer. It's either you go around the hill or you go over it. The point is; we can all get to the other side of the hill, as long as we are not lazy and we believe that we will get to where we should be. By that, nothing can stop us from getting there.

Even if you travel from where you live to a shopping mall, you will find that there are lot of ways to get to the shopping mall. There are many way to success; you can play soccer and be successful; you can play cricket and be successful; you can be a CEO and be successful; you can be a businessman and still be successful and wealthy, just like any other thing you want to pursue.

Above all, my point is this; as long as you have your mind to think, you can achieve anything you wish to achieve. It's either you are disadvantage or not, you live in the streets, you don't have parents or whatever your situation might be, the fact is; nothing can stop you to be successful and wealthy. As long as you have your mind, you can think and create your future with it.

Sometimes I ask myself, what's stopping people to achieve their goals while they still have every part of their bodies. People who are disadvantage, are using what they have to get what they want. They use their minds and their voices to create their future. They use something that you also have, but seemingly it's like something that you don't possess because you don't use your mind to better your own life; instead you use it for useless things that won't help you at all. It's either you speak something or write it down; the fact is you are creating what you are saying.

Something that is not used is worthless, but anything that is used is valuable. If you examine yourself now, are you where you want to be in life? Is your mind in harmony with what you want to achieve or against it? Do you want to stay like this for the rest of your life and watch other people succeed in front of you?

I say this is the time to get up and do something. Start now and change your life forever. Make your loved ones be proud of you and your achievements. Make your community be proud of having you. You came to this world to make a change, now is the time to make a difference and live your dream life you have always wished for; don't wait for tomorrow, but start now.

Each day gives you a blank 72 page college exercise book and a pen to write your life and your day starts immediately when you open your eyes. Now remember that this is a blank exercise book and you're the only person who can choose what to write on it.

If you wish to change your life, and become a better person than you were from yesterday, but you still write your life on this book like you did yesterday and before, this mean there is no progress in your life and you are stuck. You need a wakeup call. You have not changed anything but yet you can see that the way you were writing your life yesterday didn't help you at all.

For you to change and be a better person, you need to change what you are writing on this exercise book. You need to write things that will assist you in achieving your goals tomorrow. Don't just write one page on the exercise book and expect to achieve your goals.

Remember that you are given 72 blank pages to plan your future ahead of you, and you need to strive and write on all 72 pages. If you do this and write productive things on your book of life, you will achieve your dreams and goals in the quickest way you have never even imagine.

Make sure that you push and write whatever you can and as many pages as possible in one day. Don't wait for tomorrow because tomorrow will come with another blank 72 pages you'll need to write on.

Now as you continue to write on this book, make sure that every day you finish the day with a positive balance, not a negative balance. If you finish with a positive balance, the next day you will start with a positive balance and that will be your advantage on every day.

What do I mean by all this? Picture yourself as an accounting student; you know that in every financial year the balance is brought forward to the next financial year. Same thing applies with your book of life; you cannot just finish your day with negative things each day, this will result to the failure of not achieving your goals in life. You will start your next day with a negative balance and it will become increasingly difficult to finish with a positive balance.

If you finish your days with a negative balance, you will never make it in achieving your goals because you will also start your next day with a negative balance brought forward, plus it will be difficult for you to end that day on a positive balance.

You just cannot bring hatred and gossiping about other people to your next day and expert to finish your day on a positive balance. You need to forgive yourself and everyone that did you wrong that same day, so you won't start on a negative balance. You need to stop gossiping about other people because that alone takes a lot of your time and you investing it on someone else.

There are a lot of things I can continue to count, but I only choose these two as an examples. The fact is; all those negative things which you know about should stop now. They are just waste of your own precious time that can never be replaced. Don't do things like gossiping and you should be a forgiving person; because if you look at it, the time you hate someone, you only hurt yourself while that person is busy at the beach having fun with his/her friends.

Focus on yourself and start your day on a positive balance and also finish it on a positive balance. By doing this, you are only helping yourself and you'll start to see good things flowing into your life. Start your day by being grateful for waking up and for everything that you see around you.

Be happy and grateful for everything you can think off and start your day on a positive balance. And also by doing this, you already giving yourself a go ahead and by the time you start doing what you normally do in the morning, you already one step ahead, plus the positive balance that is brought forward from the previous day. At this time you are already a winner and nothing can stop you in achieving anything that you desire.

Ok, instead of Joseph in the biblical times let's take a look at another person who is currently alive in this time of life, our South African president Jacob Zuma. Now this is a man who was in prison for years before South Africa was a free country. This man had to suffer before he went to prison and during his incarceration just because he was fighting for all South African to be free.

But through all those suffering he had one thing in mind, he knew where he was going too and he already had seen the end result before the apartheid was over. Now President Zuma comes from a very poor environment and most people had something to say about him before he was president.

I don't know the president personally and I don't know how he thought before; but through his footsteps now, it clearly shows how he thought before. Let's put aside all the negative things that we hear about him, whether they are there or not, the fact is, they won't help me or you at the end of the day. I want us to focus on the things that will help me and you succeed without fail. Now let's look on how he got to where he is now, his success.

Before Jacob Zuma was president, some people wanted him to be president and some didn't approve of him to be president and they said a lot of negative things about him. They were saying things like he is uneducated to be president and so forth. But later on he became the President of South Africa, and not only that, he came to be the president for the second term as well.

As I said before that I don't know the president personally and I also don't know the level of education he has. But the fact is, even if he is uneducated as people expect him to be, he became the president of South Africa. It is obvious that with or without education you can get to where you want to be, as long as you see yourself in the place you wish to be in.

Don't get me wrong, I'm not saying education is not important, but what I'm saying is, if you do your part as I explain in this book, you don't have to worry about how you'll get there because everything will fall into place on its own.

It is not your job to worry about how you'll get to where you are planning to be, but your job is to see yourself as you already in that place you want to be in. See the end result before you even get to where you should be and the how will come looking for you.

President Zuma knew where he was going too and he had a clear and a perfect end result for his dream. Now let me prove to you with another example that he knew where he was going too. When president Zuma was about to be president of South Africa, he was in and out of court, where criminal charges were laid against him.

He was facing real problems, but he didn't see it as problems. But as challenges which came to promote him to his next level in his life. He was famous for the song he would sing throughout all the challenges he had to face and companies were making a lot of money through the caller tunes they were selling based on this song.

He sang this song most of the time when he came out of the court when thousands of fans were waiting for him outside the court. After he delivers a speech to his fans, he would sing "Letha umshini wami, Wena uyangibambezela." It's a Zulu song which means, bring my machine, you are holding me back.

Through this song, most South Africans interpreted it as he was speaking to the president at that time, telling him to give him his position as president and to stop holding him back. Jacob Zuma knew where he was going too and he used his voice to create his future just by singing this song.

Through this song you could tell that he knew he wasn't going to prison again. He saw the end result before he was even president. And today he is still the president of South Africa for the second time. Through all the negative things that were said about him, he made sure he owned his dream. This is very important to understand, because people will always talk. It is very important for yourself to focus and not lose hope on what you want to achieve.

There are still negative things that are said about him, but if you look at those people, and where the president is right now; there is a huge gap. And do you want to know why there is a huge gap? It's because he had a dream in his mind and he doesn't allow what people say to bring him down and move him away from his dream.

So through all the negative things you have heard about him, have you ever heard him entertaining those remarks? Think about it, have you? I personally haven't heard him even once responding to the things that are said about him, and I'm sure your answer is also no. So why do you think he doesn't entertain those comments that are said about him and the pictures that they draw of him?

The answer is simple, he understands that when you are playing in a soccer match, the supporters always have something to say about you, and your only job is to focus on the ball you playing. Keep your eyes on the ball and don't take your eyes away from the ball in order to win your game.

Once you move your eyes away from the ball and respond to what your supporters are saying about you, you will lose the ball to the team you are playing against and you'll end up losing since you entertain your supporters. The rules are, to play your game and play it well without losing focus of the ball; in that way you always have a greater chance to win because you focus on what you are doing.

I personally believe that our president is using this technique and it's working for him perfectly, a technique that you can also use because it will work for you every time. I understand that some people love our president and some don't, but I suggest you don't take this personally because you can learn a thing or two from the strategy he used to get to where he is today.

My aim here in this book is to teach, show and prove to you that you can also be successful and wealthy very easily if you start controlling your mind and the words you say from today. Accept God and let Him lead and control your life.

Coming from a poor environment, the level of education he has and all the negative things that were said or being said to the president. The fact remains the same, he has been re-elected for the second term as the president of South Africa. Surely that should tell you something about him and the formula that he uses.

Take a look at where Nkosazane Dlamini Zuma is at now; she is the chairperson of the African Union. Now look where she comes from; can you see that your background can never hold you back? In fact, nothing can hold you back if you believe that you can be something.

Same applies to you. It is very important to know where you are going too, because if you don't, you will get lost along the way. When you want to go to a shopping mall, you first have to think about it, then prepare yourself for the trip, then take a taxi or drive to the shopping mall, and within 30 minutes to an hour you will arrive at the shopping mall.

You arrived at the shopping mall in 30 minutes time because you first planned to go there. Secondly, you knew where you were going too. You didn't get lost along the way and you arrived at the shopping mall in a very short period of time. But yet again, if you don't know where you going in life, you would get into a taxi or into your car and drive around for the whole year and yet you won't even get to your destination because you don't even know where you are going too.

You might even end up in a car crash and your life could be over without even reaching your destination or fulfil your purpose in life. So it is very important to know where you are going in life so you won't get lost or crash along the way; and you will be able to get to your destination in a very short period of time.

Never allow someone to discourage you by saying that you will never going to make it. Never allow someone to tell you that you can never be where you planning to be. If president Zuma and the chairperson of the African Union succeeded from where they were without being discouraged by their social background, what is stopping you? If they did it, **I CAN** do it. **YOU CAN** do it. **EVERYBODY** who has faith CAN DO. Believe that you **CAN** do it, and I believe that you **WILL** do it. Start now and you don't have to worry about tomorrow because good things will start looking for you.

Success comes from within, not in what you do. But if you're successful from within, everything that you do will become a success. I'm sure you have heard of people who had won millions from the lottery, and after one to two years all that money they had won is gone, and they are back to square one. Again there are people who inherit a large sum of money and again, in a couple of months the money is all gone, why? It's because those people were not successful from within and the money had to go away because there is no room for it in that person.

Be successful from within and you will never be broke again in your whole life. Plus if you teach this book to your kids, your family and the next generations will continue to be successful forever. Have faith in what you do, own your dream and focus on it; and use what you have to get what you want.

Do what you have to do with everything in your power right now, so you can be..., have... and do what you want to do with your whole life. To be where you want to be tomorrow you have to start now and work for the better tomorrow you wish to have.

Never ever quit. Make sure that you go ahead with your scheduled plan no matter what comes your way. You need to run and finish the race in order to win, achieve and accomplish all your desires. The only way to achieve your goals is to keep moving forward, and that is the only way you'll get where you want to be.

When you are defeated it doesn't mean that you must quit in life. It means you must go back to seek advice, to learn more technics, do some more research and counselling. Seek professional help in the field that you are dealing with. Then get back and fight with everything that you have acquired from different sources. More especially because the power to fight back lies within you. Defeat doesn't mean fail, but it means to be strong, overcome and win victories.

This reminds me of a song that is sang in many churches which goes by "There is a race that I must run, there a victories to be won, give me power every hour to be true." This song says it all and if you apply it in your life, miracles will come flowing in your presences.

Look at Joseph in the Bible, he didn't think of giving up when he was sold by his brothers. He didn't think of giving up when he was in prison for something he didn't do. He kept pushing till he became what God planned for him to be. Let's look at another person, DR. Nelson Mandela, he was also in prison for many years yet he was fighting for the people of South Africa to be free.

He never thought of giving up. He kept on pushing till God rewarded him for his hard work. You just have to push with everything that you have so you can win the race. I am also in prison, but I never thought of giving up. A lot of things happen inside this place, but I never thought of giving up.

I know where I am going and want to achieve in life, so I keep on pushing. When prisoners are sleeping at night, I am awake, writing how I want my life to be when I get out. I sleep 3-4 hours a day, not because I want too, but because I want success so bad that I can't wait for the next day to continue from where I left off.

Failure is never an option. I am already in pain by being in prison, and therefore I had to convert my pain into success and get something out of my pain. I knew that if I just sit there, I will accumulate more pain just by doing nothing, and this pain will last forever. But after I decided that I want to end the pain and bring success into my life, I took necessary actions.

People would just sit and think that I had it easy with life, but that's not true. The challenges I faced took out the best in me and I made choices that were going to change my life forever. I just couldn't stand feeling that I want to be rich but I don't do anything about it.

I couldn't just let my dream pass by and waste my life while I watch and celebrate other people's success. I also wanted to be admired and I just had to take steps in achieving what I desired to have and be. The only way you can change your current situation that you always complain about, is to stand up now and start running your race.

If you decide to stay down, you will always be down while you watch people running past you. No one can run the race for you because everyone is trying to win their own race.

When a person goes to prison most people think that life is finished and they just won't be anything in life left for that person. But if I got myself up and Mandela got himself up and Joseph got himself up, what could stop you from getting yourself up while you are even outside and not in prison?

Do you think you are being fair to yourself while you still have a chance but you are not using it? Do you think it's fair to the people who are pulling life sentence in prison for crimes they didn't do, and their chance to shine was taken away from them, while you are outside in the real world and wasting time that can never be replaced?

Would you find it better to go inside prison instead of someone who still wishes to have one chance because already you have seen yourself as a failure? What are you even planning to be in future? Where do you see yourself in 5 or 10 years? Still complaining that life is unfair?

What are you doing to change your life? Do you think it's fair to people who are physically disadvantaged while you have everything and you don't even appreciate what you have. Is something useful to you when it's not being used? Why can't you just give your body parts to the people who are in need of them most and can make full use of them?

You have everything in your hands but you still find life unfair? You still have the brain to think with, but you choose to think about useless things that will never help you. If something is not helping you, leave it and change to something else.

The method you applied few months back, if it didn't help you, use some alternative methods that will assist you to achieve your goals in the future. Just recently, I was talking with an ex-girlfriend of my friend and unfortunately they broke up.

She is telling me that she sees no point in living just because of a man she was not even married too. This young woman is even in her early twenties but she thinks like this now. She has not been doing anything about her life and sitting and praying that my friend will marry her one day, while she can't even take care of herself.

How can a man marry you while you can't take care of yourself and your own life? That alone shows that you won't take care of him or his children because you can't even take care of yourself. I personally wouldn't want to marry a woman who will just sit there and expect hand out all the time.

Those times are over and women out there are doing something about their lives. I respect the ladies who are in control, strong and enjoying the life journey. Yes, as a man I should be a provider for my lady and family, but what will I be rewarding you for if you can't even wash your own clothes?

As my friend's ex-girlfriend was talking to me and asking for solutions, I thought to myself that this woman can't even cook, yet she is expecting to be married. And when I told her to think of a solution, she is telling me she can't think for herself and I should think for her.

Like WOW! Can you just imagine a young woman talking like this, saying that she can't think for herself? And so she expects me to jump into her brain and think for her. My brothers and sisters, what I'm saying here is that the fact that you still alive and breathing means that you can still make it far in life.

You can even be a millionaire tomorrow if you can only apply what's needed to be applied today. People must stop thinking that everything will always stay the same, because it won't. Everything on earth is changing; even the earth is moving to show us that we too should keep moving forward.

You need to get up now and do something with your life so you can be successful. We all need to be successful so we could change the world into a better place. If you don't play your part in this world, no one else will play it for you. You are the one who can be the best player that can ever be, not somebody else, but you. Get up and play your part.

What happens tomorrow is completely up to you, and it's all based on what you do today. Proverbs 15:6 will tell you that good people will start to be wealthy and successful in everything that they do, only because good people attracts good things into their lives.

But wicked people will attract trouble till they don't have anything left, why? Because of the law of attraction, you reap what you sow. If you want to be broke, continue or start to be a wicked person, but if you want to be successful and wealthy you need to be a good person so you will attract all good things into your life. Allow every good thing to flow at all times into your presence.

When you respect your God and keep His Laws at all times, you and your whole family and the next generations to come will keep on being successful and wealthy (Deuteronomy 5:29). When you keep the Laws of

God and everything that I'm explaining here in this book, only abundance of success and wealthy will keep flowing into your life and you will be blessed beyond measure.

Now let me tell you how we people view life. Suppose you are watching a soccer match and your favourite team is playing in the finals. How do you feel from the beginning of the match throughout the game and no goals have been conceived? You feel nervous, worried and you have fear of losing the game. But what happens if the other team scores first and your favourite team is losing? You get more nervous and worried because you already feel that your team is losing the game and your fear increases as well. So even in life, when you are in trouble and challenges have surrounded you, you feel nervous, worried and you have fear of looking ahead.

You just feel like it's the end of the world, and you feel like life is not worth living anymore. But what happens if your favourite team scores first? Obviously you feel happy, a bit relaxed and you feel like your team is winning the game more especially towards the end of the soccer match. But yet again, how would you really feel when you watch the replay of the whole match after your team had won?

Obviously you know that your favourite team had already won the game and you just want to watch the replay of it, since you recorded the match. And now your feelings will change when you watching the game for the second time and you just know what will happen next? Of course this time you won't be nervous, worried or have fear of losing the game because you already know the outcome of the soccer match and you just feel relaxed.

Now this is the way I want you to feel after you finish reading this book. I'll need you to be relaxed, like you are living your life for the second time and you just know everything that is going to happen next. But the difference is that, this time I will be giving you instructions and a map to follow which will help you to get to your destination faster and safely.

This map I'm giving you will make sure that you don't get lost along the way and do the mistakes that you did before, but it will show you everything that you need in order to get where you want to be in life. This will only happen if you follow all the instructions accordingly to this book you are reading now.

This time you won't have any fears or worries because failure won't even be an option; but only success and happiness in your whole life is ahead of you. This time you are living your life like the replay of the soccer match you are watching.

You should feel relaxed and happy because you know for sure that you will win and be successful. The only difference is that I am giving you the instructions, a manual and a lifetime study guide which will guide and bring you anything and everything you have ever desired in your whole life. This time you will write your own life with a conscious mind and only abundance of wealthy and success is coming your way from today.

Talk to God at all times, He is right inside you. Ask and pray for everything that you wish to have or change and when you do this, He will answer all your prayers. Doesn't the scripture tell you to ask for anything and your request or prayer will be answered?

I have shown you already that the Bible tells you to ask for anything and your prayers will be answered, in this way you'll be honouring God and you will be successful in everything that you do (Proverbs 16:3).

Listen to me; when you are super wealthy you have already built a strong defence against any attack that might come to you, and you will be protected because of your wealth. But when you are broke and poor there is no protection at all for you.

Listen my brothers and sisters, I'm not taking this statement from my head, it's written in your Bible that you carry with you all the time, or the same Bible you normally look at and say this book won't help me. I'm telling you, everything is there, go to Proverbs 10:15 and see for yourself.

This verse will tell you straight that if you are broke and poor, you are not protected at all. People who have money will get to use you anyhow because they have something that you don't have. You will complain but there's nothing you can do because they are going to pay you that little amount of money for doing what you don't want to do.

People with money will make sure they will use you in a way that you will even regret what you did with them or for them. And the fact about this is that you will keep doing what you don't like every day because you don't have the money. Unless you take my advice and listen to my words, you can change your tomorrow by the decision you'll make now.

When will you stop complaining about what's being done to you? When will you stop complaining that your boss doesn't like you and he/she is ill-treating you? He/she will continue to do that because you don't have what you need, and he/she has what you need, even though it's not enough for you at all.

When will you stop complaining? When will the change take place? Why are you even allowing it to happen to you daily? Why are you wasting your precious time that can never be replaced? Do you understand how much of time you are wasting from your life, plus it keeps on happening to you because all your focus is on your challenges or complains?

Do you even understand that you are allowing it to keep happening to you because of your sorrows, feeling sorry for yourself? So tell me my brother/sister what will you do from now onwards to change all of this?

When will you stop complaining? I'm telling you that you'll stop complaining when you start to take actions on what I'm explaining and teaching you to practise. It's so amazing because it has always been in front of you.

The Bible tells you right away that you need to be rich so you won't allow other people to control your life. Automatically when you are wealthy you take control of everything; you start to be happy, you take your kids to the best schools, you spoil your parents with goodies and live the life like you should have been all these years.

When you are wealthy you can even help people and serve God through His people. But you cannot do this in a way that will satisfy you if you don't have enough money. Yes you can serve God and the people with your time, but it will not be enough. You'll need money to complete your desires when it comes to helping the people of your community and making a change in people's lives forever. You need to start now and make a change on the outside by what you think and produce from the inside.

You must know that life is like a chess game, once you touch the chess piece you should move that piece you have already touched. The rule is simple, a touch is a move. Even if you touch the piece by mistake and you wanted to play another one, you just cannot play another one except to play the piece you already touched.

Since you have made your choice and touched the piece, you just cannot change your move, but you have to suffer the consequences of the touch you made. And that move you are going to make next can cost you to loss the whole game. So even in our lives, we live our daily lives with this rule, a touch is a move. Once you do something like hitting someone with a stick, you just cannot take it back because you have already made your move and you have beaten that person.

Even if that person was wrong or right and you have beaten him badly, you should live with what you have done and suffer the consequences that will follow after your actions. Even when you say something bad like swearing someone, you can't take your words back, except to reap what you have already sown.

Now in this book I am showing you which piece to move before you even touch any piece, so you can win the game with no mistakes done. But if you have already done some mistakes, that's still ok because you are reading this book just in the right time, while you still have a chance to rectify your mistakes that you have done.

I'm telling and showing you on how to fix the mistakes you had already done so you can win your game you playing. Take this book as your number one coach and definitely sure you will win your game because you have the best coach. Take your life like a game of chess and this book as your coach and surely you won't make any mistakes till you win your game and be successful and wealthy from today.

You know that when you completely obey your God and His Laws, He will make you very successful and wealthy in everything that you do (2 Kings 18:6-7). Hezekiah was also successful because he followed the Laws, and you too can be successful if you follow the Laws; and God has made it very easy for us because He has written them in our hearts and minds.

Again my brothers and sisters, I must inform you that you have a choice and everything is up to you now. Your mind has become conscious and everything is entirely up to you. Now what will be your next move?

When you think about good things, the Lord your God will bless you and make you successful in what you desire. Again if you think about evil things, the Lord your God will curse you because of your evil thoughts. But when you hear God's Laws and apply them to your life, He will bless you with everything beyond measure (Deuteronomy 11:26-27).

It's even worse to us men; you just cannot be a poor man. How would you provide for your woman or family if you are broke? If you are a man, you should really be wealthy so you can provide, and you need to work for your wealth from the inside till the outside (Proverbs 11:16). Napoleon Hill was right when he said, "Think and grow rich". When you think about wealth and take necessary actions, you just cannot be broke, but you'll be blessed with success beyond measure.

If you are a fool, you won't think and grow rich. You will only think about stupid things which will keep recurring in your life. But when you accomplish all your desires, you will feel good and every good thing will continue to look for you wherever you are (Proverbs 13:19); feel good and allow good things to flow into your life; this is the Law.

Let me show you again in the book of Psalms 1:2-3, that you attract everything you are, to you; and that is why they say like attracts like. All the happiness and joy you need is in the Laws of your God. Think and meditate on them every time of the day and you will be drawing success and prosperity into your life. It's so simple don't you think?

Throughout the book I am mentioning the principles that will make you successful and wealthy from today, and it is God's Laws. Now these people who think and meditate on the Laws will be like trees growing nearby the river, and these trees produces fruits and they always have leaves. These people prosper and succeed in everything that they do.

If you follow God's Laws, you will prosper and make a change in this world. But if you don't follow these Laws, you will continue to be broke, poor and think money is evil and the Lord doesn't approve of someone having a lot of money. Meanwhile the Lord God wants everybody to be rich so we can help and serve the people who are struggling. You decide now if you want to be rich and live a comfortable life, or if you want to continue to be broke and allow people who have money to control you and your life. The choice is yours after all.

Everything starts privately, from within, so you could be celebrated in public, on the outside when everyone is watching. Eric Thomas once said; "If you want success, you got to want it like you want to breathe."

Eric understood that when you under the water, there is nothing else you want to do except to breath and get air. If however you don't get the air you need, you will eventually die. Same principle should be applied in your life, when you know that being broke is going to kill you. You need to purse success and fight for it.

If you have seen someone on asthma attack or you have been on asthma attack, you will relate better to this. When the attack has come, you forget about everything and you just need air and you want to breathe properly.

I personally know and understand how an asthma attack works because for thirteen years I have had asthma, and I would get an attack now and again. Every single month an ambulance would come to pick me up at home and take me to the hospital when things went bad. I only needed to breath and nothing else.

My father even bought an asthma machine to use at home when the attack struck again. You cannot even walk when it's bad, and that's how bad it is to have an asthma attack. Now, when you want success as you want to breathe, you forget about everything else that is going on around you and you focus on what you need. If you really want success that bad, you will obtain it. When you draw closer to success, it will draw closer to you. This is just the law and it always works.

If you relax while being broke, it will eventually kill you. But why not try to fight and be successful? What is there that you will lose because you're already broke and it's killing you? Rather fight for success because you might win, and when you win all the pain and suffering you are in right now will be gone forever.

You need to purse success at all times. When you pursue to be successful and you really want to be successful like you want to breathe when you are pressed underneath the water; you will need a plan to escape the pressure that is exerted upon you. An errand of mercy should be applied and how to accomplish and activate everything successfully. Now, without that kind of plan, how would you know where you have started, where your voyage is taking you too, and how you'll get there? Therefore, you need a map.

We were all created equally, whether from a rich or poor family, but the fact remains that we were all created equally. The successful people worked hard in private so they could be celebrated in public. Musicians make music in private so they could be celebrated in public.

Chapter 5
STOP BEING IN YOUR OWN PRISON, JUST FORGIVE & HEAL YOUR LIFE

You don't have to be in prison to be a prisoner, but you can be a prisoner anywhere you are with the sufferings and misery you withhold deep inside you. The things you think about and talk about will show if you are a prisoner or a free man/woman. You have to let your old ways go so you can be free.

In the book of Job 16:8, Job said he is a prisoner, yet he was not in prison. This clearly tells us that you don't have to be a prisoner only because you are inside the prison walls. I don't understand why people think that you have to be in a correctional centre and be incarcerated in order to be a prisoner.

Bear in mind that we a spiritual beings and the toughest prisoner you could ever be is to be a prisoner spiritually, emotionally and mentally; to top it all people have imprison themselves to life imprisonment and no correctional centre can set you free unless you set yourself free from your own prison.

Paul and Silas were praying and worshiping God, then suddenly an earthquake shook the prison. The doors and chains were opened (Acts 16:25-26). This shows the power of praying and worshiping your God. When you do it whole heartedly everything is possible and you can open every door with your prayer. Your prayer is the only thing that could set you free from the prison you are in. When you start praying and requesting now, you can change your current moment and free yourself.

When you use these Laws or teaching I'm providing to you today, you will be like Jehoiachin, a man who was in prison for thirty-seven years. But by the time he was released from prison by the new King, he enjoyed life more than many persons, and he was also paid an allowance on a daily bases to use it as he pleases (Jeremiah 52:31-34).

Now what are you waiting for? Start applying what I have already told you in the chapters before so you can also be free and be paid an allowance every day to use anyhow. Free yourself from your own prison by using the information that is gathered in this book. I wrote this book while I'm in prison, but my mind is not imprisoned. As a spiritual person I am free and I will always be free, no matter what are the circumstances.

As I said in the previous chapter that some people who are in power and have money will oppress you because you don't have anything. You will cry but no one will help you because you don't want to help yourself by changing the way you think.

While in prison, I hear a lot of bad news from the outside world. People are ill-treating each other and it is getting worse day by day. As I am feeling the pain that the people of our Lord God are suffering, I thought to myself that the dead are better off than the living (Ecclesiastes 4:1-2).

When you go into prison, people write you off and regard you as a dead person. But what they really don't know is that, (being dead, as they regard us); we are the people who are really better than them and we are alive because some of us had accepted and allowed God to direct our lives. Notwithstanding people who are outside, are the real prisoners of their minds and they won't even be free anytime soon, if only they will ever be.

Even some people who attend a church service every week will still remain prisoners because they are failing to do one simple thing which is the key to everything and that is to **forgive** themselves and the people around them.

I regard the prison as a hospital. Some people recover and some don't. Your mind can only make you better or make you dead. The judge had to hospitalise me because he saw that I need hospitalisation. He saw that I needed to be sent to a hospice because I was very ill and I couldn't stay with the people outside.

I was regarded as a person who cannot live with the community and I needed to be taken in, with the hope that I will recover from the sickness or the disease that had already got in me. My sickness was inserted in me by the people around me and the things I was eating throughout my childhood. Everything that I had already eaten and inserted in my body was growing inside me while I wasn't aware. When the disease had to strike, I couldn't control it (wrong choice when making decisions).

It was already bigger than me and was powerful because I stored it in the inside and it grew from the inside. When it wanted to come out, it did come out and I couldn't control what's on the outside, because the inside is bigger than the outside.

Now I urge you not to go through this root I took. Don't go to prison or be a prisoner of your own thoughts. I'm giving you a way that will set you free at all times and it will be a very wise move to take my advice.

Yes, I'm a product of the prison and everything I know today I couldn't have known if I didn't go to prison, but it doesn't mean that you'll also know the things that I know if you apply to go to prison with what you are feeding in your mind. Plus there is no need to go through the pain I went through because I am sharing the information with you right now. Be a free person from today and start to fly now.

After realising the power that I have inside me, God took His place and He was working in me. In all the challenges I went through I confessed the wrong that I did to Him. I repented and forsook all the evil I use to do. And God showed me the way to live. I spoke the truth about Him and I did what was right, and everything just fell into place (2 Corinthians 6: 5-7).

Remember now, as you are sitting in that prison of yours, you may think that God is a fool. Let me inform you that He is wiser than you are. When you think God is weak, He is stronger than you are. He is the only one who can set you free, if only you start to work with Him now (1 Corinthians 1:25-26).

Now let's look at a successful and wealthy man who was also in prison for many years and he was also similar to Joseph. This is a man I'm sure you are going to like because he is or was an international icon, the late president DR. Nelson Mandela.

After Mandela was sentenced to life imprisonment he still saw the light and he knew that one day he will be outside the prison walls and the whole of South Africa will be a free country. During the hardship he went through while he was in prison, he still had faith and he had seen the end result of the South African freedom long before he was even sentenced.

I'm sure he saw the end result even before he joined the African National Congress. And by the time he joined the ANC, he had hope, together with **faith** that one day South Africa would be a free country. This is just one of the basic rules, to see the end result before you even start and by doing so you already starting to create it for yourself.

If you want to be a president, you need to see yourself as a president and live in that moment like you are already the president. Then your next step is to take necessary actions to become a president one day. DR. Mandela took action by joining the ANC, and bear in mind that by this time he had already seen the end result and the action that he took was going to turn his end result into reality.

If you want to be a millionaire, see yourself as a millionaire and live in that moment like you already a millionaire. If you want to be a hero, see yourself as a hero and live in that moment like you are already a hero and take necessary actions to turn your dreams into a reality.

Just set your mind on anything you want to be and live in that moment and also by doing so you are creating your dream to come looking for you. Then by taking action you are meeting your dream half way and turning it into reality.

Now before DR. Nelson Mandela was released from prison, he was already a successful man. He started to live comfortably than before, while he was still in prison. And by the time he was released from prison, his success, wealth and dreams was already waiting for him. When DR. Mandela spoke to the people he was leading, he spoke about **forgiving** and making peace in one of his speeches. He had forgiven the people who took away 27 years of his life. These are the same people who took away his right to be a husband, a father, and they also made him suffer in prison for all this time, through hard labour and many things that happen inside the prison walls.

Even after elections when he became the president of South Africa, he didn't want to revenge in any form though he had powers too. Mandela was a very wise man who understood that a country can never go forward without forgiving. Mandela knew and understood that forgiving was the key to everything and without it, you just cannot move forward.

Now this is a very good example and this is what really made DR Mandela one of the powerful presidents in the whole world. He was not powerful because he was in prison for 27 years, no, but he was powerful because he forgave the people who took his life away from him and his family.

Around those years when the former president of the United State of America asked DR Mandela if he still hates the people who took away his life, and his response was, "I hate them, but if I continue to hate them I would still be a prisoner in my mind. They might have taken away my life, but I refuse to allow them to take away my mind as well."

This clearly tells us that Mandela was a very wise man after all, and that he made a good decision by forgiving. Do you honestly think that DR Mandela would have been so much powerful and successful if he didn't forgive the people who took away his life? I personally don't think so, and I'm sure most people would agree with me. Everything comes back to one key word which is **"FORGIVENESS."** Forgive and let miracles flow into your life.

Now this is why you'll find people who are not in prison suffering mentally and emotionally; it's because they don't want to forgive and let go. In fact these types of people are in prison and they are prisoners of their minds. Now tell me, are you also in prison?

Think about it. How did you end up in where you are? How long do you want to stay there? Do you want to be free or release yourself? Do you want success to come looking for you now? So what are you waiting for? Let it go and allow all good things flow into your direction.

There is no correctional centre or minister that can set you free or put you on parole, because this is an inner prison and you are the only one who can attend to this matter. No one can set you free unless you help yourself and set your mind and yourself free by forgiving yourself and everyone that has hurt you before. I know it's hard because I have been there, but this is the only way you can heal your life and yourself and move forward. You will never move forward in life unless you start forgiving everything and everyone around who wronged you.

If you forgive someone, you are not helping them, but you are helping yourself and healing your life. Forgiving is everything and the key to everything. No matter what has the person done to you, you need to forgive, release and let go so you can move on. With forgiving, you will never go wrong.

Have you ever seen a person who is always angry and says bad things about other people progressing in life? No, I don't think you have. Do you want to know why? It's because that person has created a path of bad things only to come to him/her.

If you say something bad about someone or directly to him/her, you are basically saying that thing to yourself since we are all connected, and that very same thing you said will come directly into your life. But if you say something good to a person, again you are saying that good thing to yourself. What you think or say to somebody else is directly being said to your own life and will be manifested in future.

Joseph forgave his brothers and he was successful in everything that he did. Nelson Mandela forgave all the people who made him suffer for many years and he became successful. I personally forgave myself for everything that I have done to myself and I was free mentally, spiritually and emotionally.

I became successful in everything that I did. Forgiving yourself is very important in your life and plays a big role in healing your life. If you have done yourself wrong and did things that you are not pleasant about, you need to forgive yourself so you can move on with your life.

You too can start forgiving everything and everyone around you including yourself, so you can be successful in everything that you do. If you pray the prayer "Our father, which art in heaven," which is found in the book of Matthew 6:9-13; I'm sure you also say the part which says, "Forgive us our trespasses as we forgive those who trespass against us."

You should really mean and do what you say and start forgiving people so you can heal your life. You should stop lying to God and practice what you preach. No matter what a person has done to you, you should forgive and release the pain so you can move on and let success flow into your life.

Have you ever wondered why do most people go to church for help concerning their lives? These people are emotionally, mentally and spiritually sick. They need divine intervention in their lives. They have come to the right spiritual hospital. Some of these spiritual diseases that affect their lives are as follows:

Filthy thoughts, immoral ways, shameful deeds, practise witchcraft, hate others; they are hard to get along with, jealous, angry, and selfish. They not only argue and cause trouble, but they are envious. They get drunk, carry on at wild parties, and do other evil things as well.

For these diseases to be treated, you must make a decision so that the power that is within you can be stimulated. The problem that you have is within you and it only needs you to attend too it, and no one else will do it for you. Even your pastor cannot help you if you don't want to help yourself by forgiving and letting go of the pain inside your heart.

You are the only doctor to your heart and no one else. You need to start servicing your client (your heart) to your best abilities and heal your client. If you don't start to forgive people today, your hatred will hold you back and you won't move forward with your life.

Again the same thing happened in my life. I didn't move forward because I still had hatred deep down in my heart.

But as soon as I started to forgive my father and forgive myself, I began to see a huge change in my life. All my life, was only the forgiving part which was holding me back after all.

This is the same principle that is applying in your life as well. You might be doing everything right, but the fact that you still holding grudges, planning to revenge one day and you still have hatred in your heart. This is the thing that will always hold you back in your life.

You can never go forward because you are holding yourself back. Success and wealth is waiting for you to release all the anger and pain you have deep down in your heart. You need to start forgiving now and release all the unnecessary things you don't need in your life.

You need to welcome success into your life by forgiving everything and everyone around you dead or alive. This is the key to everything and if you start practising it today, your life will never be the same and you will be glad that you did. Change now and set yourself free.

Let me give you are **prayer for forgiveness** you should pray on a daily bases.
"You are kind, God!
Please have pity on me.
You are always merciful!
Please wipe away my sins.
Wash me clean from all
sins and guilt.
I know about my sins,

and I can't forget
my terrible guilt.
You are really the one
I have sinned against;
I have disobeyed you
and have done wrong.
So it is right and fair for you
to correct and punish me.
I have sinned and done wrong
since the day I was born.
But you want complete honesty,
so teach me true wisdom.
Wash me with hyssop
until I am clean
and whiter than snow.
Let me be happy and joyful!
You crushed my bones,
now let them celebrate.
Turn your eyes from my sin
and cover my guilt.
Create pure thoughts in me
and make me faithful again.
Don't chase me away from you
or take your Holy Spirit
away from me.
Make me as happy as you did
when you saved me;

make me want to obey!
I will teach sinners Your Laws,
and they will return to you.
Keep me from any deadly sin.
Only You can save me!
Then I will shout and sing
about your power to save.
Help me speak,
and I will praise you, Lord.
Offerings and sacrifices
are not what you want.
The way to please you
is to feel sorrow
deep in our hearts.
This is the kind of sacrifices
You won't refuse.
Please be willing, Lord,
to help the city of Zion
and to rebuild its walls.
Then you will be pleased
with the proper sacrifices,
and we will offer bulls
on your altar once again."
(Psalms 51:1-19)

Forgiving is so powerful that it opens closed doors when
it's applied properly.

Now let me tell you a short story I witness as I'm still in prison. There were two guys playing in the courtyard, but the playing ended up in a fight. One of them was my neighbour and he had tripped the other guy and he fell badly and hurt his arm.

The other prisoners started laughing at him, while he went and called the prison warders. He then proceeded to the hospital, and also opened a case against my neighbour who tripped him. He was not even badly hurt, just a small scratch on his elbow. He also had a date to go home to his wife and kids.

Then as always, some other prisoners entertained the guy who pressed charges and told him to continue with the case and he must not drop the charges. The police came to the prison and took statements than my neighbour was arrested and locked in his room, and also attended a court case.

He asked for forgiveness from the guy who was hurt but this guy didn't forgive him at all. Even our unit manager intervened when my neighbour asked for forgiveness, but this guy made him a fool. He acted like he was forgiving him and he will drop the charges when they get to court, but he never did and the case continued. Till eventually my neighbour also opened a case against the guy who he had tripped. He said that the guy who was hurt had started hitting him first, than he tripped him. Again the police came to the prison and took statements and this other guy was also arrested and locked up in his room.

Bear in mind that he has a date to go home to see his family for good. So now two cases were opened, the only thing that was left is for them to go on trial in court with each of these guys and some witnesses.

As they were in and out of court, the day of the other guy came and he was supposed to go home, but the prison couldn't let him go home because there was a case opened against him. So now this guy was forced to come back to my neighbour and ask for forgiveness from him.

Bear in mind that the guy who is asking for forgiveness now, didn't want to forgive my neighbour in the first place. If he had forgiven him in the first place, they wouldn't be in all this mess they both are in. Just imagine coming back to ask for forgiveness to a person you didn't want to forgive.

The guy was still in prison and his not with his family where he should be, just because he didn't want to forgive. He was not even hurt badly, but through his hatred and pain that he possessed in his heart, he had to stay in prison with us while he was supposed to be home.

For years he was not with his family, but he decided to spend more time in prison because of his unforgiving heart. Luckily my neighbour was willing to forgive this guy even though he didn't forgive him at first, but the problem was that the prison won't just let this guy go home. They had to wait for the court date first so they both can withdraw their cases that they opened against each other.

The guys who were entertaining the guy who open the case first were not there to help him now as he couldn't go home. The friends were there to push everything in the beginning, but they were not there at the end to pick him up and help him. Extra days he spent with us only because he didn't want to forgive. He had to wait for the case to be withdrawn from court till he was sent outside to his family.

The thing that stopped this guy from going home was not to forgive. His heart wasn't right, and so he attracted only bad things to follow towards him. I tell you my brothers/sisters, forgiving everything and everyone around you is the **key** to everything.

Do you think any kind of relationship would be a healthy relationship without forgiveness? The answer is no. A relationship would never have a way forward without forgiving each other. If you had not forgiven your child after he/she misbehaves, how do you think that relationship would be?

You can't even imagine it because it's quite impossible don't you think? Even if you don't forgive your partner you are in love with, can you imagine how many boyfriends or girlfriends you would have had by now? It would just be a terrible experience which you don't want to face.

Changing so many partners in times like these is not healthy at all. There are a lot of different types of sexual transmitted diseases (STD's), and by not forgiving your partner you'll be harming yourself at the end because you might infect yourself from somewhere if you revenge. But if you gave in the first time, you would have protected yourself. Maybe some of you have been through what I'm talking about already and it just brings tears in your eyes when you think about it.

When you don't forgive somebody, at first you think you are doing the right thing and protecting yourself. On contrary that's not true, because you are actually harming yourself. But when you forgive, you are protecting yourself from the harmful diseases you might get. Remember, forgiving is the key to all things.

Ephesians 4:26 tells you that if you get angry, you are being pushed to make a sin. But if you are wise enough, you won't go to bed angry. Stop being angry, wrath, bitter, clamour and cruel to each other. If you apply all of this to other people, you also placing it on your life and only bad things will come following you. Also don't be rude and speak evil things about each other (Ephesians 4:31). But instead be peacemakers and be kind to one another. Make sure you forgive one another as God has forgiven you too (Ephesians 4:32).

There are people who didn't forgive people who are in prison for what they did to them or their loved ones. At the end of the day you are still the one who is feeling the pain. You need to forgive and heal that sore because no doctor can assist you with it; therefore it's in the inside and not on the outside. You need to close that door of hatred and open a better door of love.

You are not helping the other person by doing so, but you are helping yourself and clearing the entire negativity and allowing the good and positive things to find you. Through the love path you have created for yourself, nothing is impossible. Learn to forgive so you will see miracles happening in your life. Do it now and heal yourself and your life.

Some things will never ever contribute again in our lives and we just need to release them and let go so we can allow things that we are going to use to come into our lives. You need to let go of the things that you don't need in the future, but only allow the things that will assist you further into our life journey.

Let me tell you something. I have a scar on my hand, not because someone stabbed me, but it's because of what I did to that somebody; stabbing him with a broken beer bottle. All the pain I wanted this guy to feel as I was stabbing him also came back to me as the blood was running out of my hand as well.

There are even people who are in prison, not because they were the ones who were wrong in the first place, but it's because of the wrong choices they made after what had happened to them. The pain that they wanted to send out came back to them multiplied.

There are people who are in prison only because they didn't want to forgive somebody for what they did. So they decided to revenge for themselves, but also landed themselves in prison. Now since those people are in prison, who do you think is feeling the pain now?

Can you see how painful it gets if you don't forgive? Maybe you are also one of the people who are waiting to revenge on somebody. Think of the outcome first, maybe that person can hurt you even more than the pain you are feeling now. Just think about it. Let it go, because releasing whatever you have inside right now will only heal you, not to harm you like what you are planning to do.

Revenge is a dangerous motive and has never been the best idea to go with, because the pain you want to send out might come back to you doubled or tripled the pain. Don't create a path of anger and fighting back because it will hold you back to accomplish your dreams. Have the heart of forgiving before you even hurt yourself indirectly.

Now let me tell you a summarized testimonial about myself; about my upbringing, going to prison and being where I am today.

In 2012 I caught my girlfriend with my cousin in the same room and they were both naked. I was drunk and also high on drugs, and I acted without thinking. I started beating both of them, but my cousin managed to escape. I then continued beating my girlfriend up until I had enough of beating her and I left the house. The following day I heard that she was admitted in hospital and in the ICU.

I was still drunk and high at that time and I couldn't believe what I was hearing. I then took myself to the police station and I was arrested. The following day unfortunately my girlfriend passed away. I was still in the police custody at that time and I was going to attend court the following morning.

Everything happened fast and I had no intention of killing my girlfriend, as I didn't use any kind of weapon except for my hands and feet. Before I went to the police station I had already called my girlfriend's mother to apologies and she informed me on how bad was the situation on her daughter's life.

So during the two days I was in the police custody, I was praying day and night for my girlfriend to survive and not to die, but that didn't happen. I had already created what had happen 10 days before, and praying in the police station as I was arrested was not going to help after all.

I got bail, and later pleaded guilty for my actions. I was sentenced to 10 years imprisonment with 2 years suspended, and I had to go through a horrible experience since I have never been to prison before. Then while I was in prison and serving my years I continued drinking alcohol and taking drugs like I did before when I was still outside.

Now let me tell you how I created what I went through with what I said. About 10 days before the incident took place. My girlfriend called me and told me that she was visiting her relatives in another city. Then about two hours later I received a call from one of my friends telling me that he saw my girlfriend somewhere drinking alcohol with some other guys.

He asked me if he could come and fetch me so I could see this myself, since they have been drinking in the same spot for hours. This showed that they had been busy enjoying themselves until the following day without sleeping. And he could tell that they are still planning not to sleep that day, as my friend told me. I was also drunk and I told my friend that I can't go there because I'm afraid of what I could do there, rather just let it go.

Two days later another friend of mine came to where I live and he was also drunk. He told me he was out partying somewhere and he saw my girlfriend with other men and he took her by force from those guys. My friend told me that I should go to his car that was parked just outside my gate while he entered inside the house.

When I got to the car, I couldn't even recognise my girlfriend. But when I looked closely I saw that it was my girlfriend and she was with her friend. They both came inside the house with me and I had a chat with my girlfriend. I asked her why did she lied to me that she was out of town because she knew that I know a lot of people who were going to tell me when they saw her somewhere, since everyone knew that she was my girlfriend. I continued to tell her that what she did was wrong and one day if something like this could ever happen, **I would kill her and I would go to prison after killing her**.

Then 8 days later, the day of the incident, my girlfriend was supposed to be with me. So as I was drunk and high with some of my friends, I missed my girlfriend and I wanted to be with her. I called her on her phone but her cell phone was off. Then I told myself that she is playing hide and seek and she was really testing me if I'm that well-known in my city or if I could just find her.

I proceeded to her home, but I didn't find her. I made one phone call and I went to see the person who told me where she was. I went to the house where my girlfriend was, and I already knew that she was with my cousin. I also know that they knew each other because in most cases they were always with me at my place when we were having fun with lot of people. So when I got to the house I didn't think I would find the situation as it was. I thought that I was going to find them having fun like we always used to do, and I would have just joined them in enjoying ourselves; but I was fooling myself.

I went inside the house and saw some people who were also drunk and sleeping in the dining room, but I could not see my cousin or my girlfriend. I proceeded to the bedroom where I found both of them in that room. And what I had created 8 days ago with my voice and emotions was going to take place. There is no one to blame except for myself. If I didn't say what I said before, that day I was facing, nothing would have taken place. I created my future and it was only me to be blamed for everything.

The moment I spoke those words, I never knew that I was creating what I was saying. I thought I was not a criminal because I didn't break in people's houses or steal from them, but I was only fooling myself. I was really a criminal all this time since I was using drugs. The minute

I took the drugs, I was a criminal and applying to go to prison from the outcome of the drugs I used. I just didn't see that something would ever take me to prison, but I was only fooling myself.

Now how did I get myself into prison? The answer is simple, by what I **said** with very strong **emotions** of anger. I had already created my fate from the inside, and nothing was going to change what I had already said. The only thing that was left was for what I have said to take place. I didn't have to know **how** it was going to happen, but since I had create what I said, the **how** was going to take care of itself.

Psalms 141:3 is a prayer for the Lord's protection to help me to guard my words whenever I speak, but I chose not to guard what I said because I didn't understand the power of the tongue. Yet Matthew 12:36 tells me that I will have to account for every careless word I have spoken. But still, I didn't know this and I never took notice. All this time the truth about life and how I'm supposed to live it has always been there, but I chose to ignore it. The Bible was there to guide me and give me wisdom, but I was too busy with my life that I didn't worry myself in reading and understanding the scriptures.

Just like Proverbs 18:20-21 says, if I made my words good, I was going to be glad, but since I choose to use my words in a negative way, I had to suffer the consequences. I didn't bring life with my words, but I brought death; and I had to eat everything that I said with the actions that I took.

All my life I have been missing my parent's love. My mother passed away early, but my father didn't care on how I survive even though I was living with him in the same house. I even neglected all my kids and I didn't love them because I didn't know what love was since I wasn't getting it as well from my father. I was then introduced in hustling and I didn't care at all for my kids. I had to look for love in the wrong places and I hated my father so much for what he did to me over the years. I did a lot of bad things just to survive and be like every other teenager while he was still alive. When my father passed away I didn't feel any pain because he was like a complete stranger to me. 7 days would go past while we don't even see each other, yet we live in a three bedroom house.

After I started using my time productively in prison by reading books, I started to see a huge change in my life. These books I was reading daily were working miracles within me. I have never loved reading before and I don't know how it happened to be where I am today with reading.

I started to forgive my father for all the things he did to me or should I say the things he didn't do for me as a father, and most importantly I started to forgive myself for everything I have done to myself and I stopped blaming other people for my actions. I was the one who really made bad choices, not other people. In fact, I thank my father for everything because he made me the man I am today.

I then came to understand that I have created everything that has ever happened to my life whether it was good or bad. I never knew before that whatever I said or thought about, I was the one who was creating it to happen to me.

And it took me 763 days inside the prison walls to begin to see a huge change in my life and realise all this. I stopped taking drugs and alcohol and I knew that happiness doesn't come with these things and it doesn't start from the outside, but happiness first starts from within. I found myself and what was missing in my life. I healed myself and I healed my life. It is true that the prison doesn't change a person, but a person can only change himself by the way he thinks.

I started to be successful in everything I did, while in prison, amazing, aren't you? Yes it's true, I was and I am successful in everything that I do. Do you want to know why? It's because I allowed God to take control of my life, and He is in control.

The God that is within me is working miracles in my life. Even Genesis 39:3 tells us that the Lord was helping Joseph to be successful in everything that he did, yet he was still in prison. But I would like to tell you that I am not a prisoner because I am a Spirit and I am **FREE**.

My body is the only thing that is in prison, and I don't see the prison as a prison to me or a place which is blocking me to achieve what I want, but I see the prison as a college where God has sent me to recover my original settings that He inserted in me before I was even born. He sent me to this college because He wanted me to search and find my special gifts that He has stored within me.

He sent me to this place so I could appreciate life, cherish it and serve Him according to His Word, and the only truth. I **deserve** to be in prison for my **actions**, but it is also true that the prison is the darkest gift. In the time of my hardship, my senses became very clear on what is truly important in my life, and I strived to overcome all the unnecessary obligations. The hardship I went through introduced me to myself and I had to stand up firmly and unshakable. The same hardship roused and raised my intensity to be free, and my faith was redeemed, and all the glory goes to The Most High God.

People who are outside in the real world think that people in prison are dead, but I must tell you that this notion is not true; in fact, it's the other way around. People, who are in prison and have accepted God, are the ones that are living, but most people who are outside and haven't accepted God are the ones who are dead. Ecclesiastes 4:2 confirms my statement when it says "The dead are better off than the living."

Ephesians 2:1-10 tells me clearly that in the past I was dead because I sinned and fought against God. But God loved me so much that He made me alive through Christ. He raised me from the dead to life and I am saved through the faith I have from within me.

God planned for me to do good things, to love and serve Him truthfully through His people and to live as He has always wanted me too. I believe that if you have never been tested, you cannot be trusted; and therefore God wanted me to be tested first and go through all the trials and tribulations, so I could testify about what I know and have experienced myself.

Through my whole life, **forgiving** was the **main key to everything**. After forgiving my father and myself I started to live a very happier life than before, Matthew 6:14 also confirms my statement. Everything started to grow into place because God had also forgiven me for my sins.

While in prison (college) so to say, I didn't sit down and complain about my situation, but instead I did something to better my life and future. I personally believe in doing what you can do, with everything you have, at your current position; and that is what I did. With God directing my life, everything that I desire and pursue has already been made a success.

To tell you the honest truth, I am blessed even to be alive today because of the things I have went through. Now I can see that God had a purpose with me and He wanted to fulfil it through the journey I am going through.

Through the hatred I had for my father, he was still controlling my life even though he had passed away. I allowed the pain I had buried inside me to still control my life for a very long time. But if you look at it, I was the one who was hurting myself and not releasing the pain that I still had.

In my whole life I have been blocking and stopping all good things to come to me because I had hatred deep down in my heart. I had created a path of bad things to only come my way. Every time somebody said or did something that I didn't like, I got angry, defensive and I fight back with words or physically, all because of the hatred that I had buried alive deep down inside me as I was growing up.

Exodus 21:13 was also another verse which made me heal after beating myself up for taking someone's life while I didn't intend too. I cried a lot and I hated myself for what I did, and worse part it could never be taken back and I will have to live with the outcome of my actions for the rest of my life. You'll hear people say that a man doesn't cry, but this notion is not true. How can you heal from a terrible pain if you don't feel the pain so you could release it? If I didn't cry I was going to bury the pain inside me alive. But crying; feeling the pain and releasing it is the best way to heal you. And through accepting God as the owner and driver of my life, I accepted His Word when He said, "If I didn't plan to take someone's life, He The Most High God allowed it to happen; and I must run to a safe place that He has organised for me." And that's why it was never a hustle and hard for me to plead guilty for my action.

You'll hear people; mostly prisoners say that a crime is something that you need to deny even though you did it. On the contrary to me that wasn't the case. As the person I was really am, I couldn't deny what I did. Most importantly and something I didn't notice at that time; God had already made a plan for me in the safe place where He said I must run too, which was the prison (Numbers 35:11) and (Deuteronomy 4:43).

I accepted the punishment from the government authority, that was imposed by God to punish me for the terrible sin I had committed (Psalms 141:5). I came to realise that I had to die before I was raised to life. Lazarus had to die and go down so he could be raised to life. He was not going to be raised to life if he didn't die (John 11:38-43).

The same thing happened with me. I had to die first and go to prison so God will take His place and be raised back to life. When He shouted and said, "Lungelo, come out!" I had to listen and come out before it was too late. **You** too my brothers and sisters, come out from that prison of yours before it's too late.

God has spoken to you and you should listen before it's too late for you to come out. Maybe people will think that you will stink when you come out, but through God's perfect time, now is the time. Come out from that prison and heal your life. Work together with God and let Him touch your life and be in control so you can activate what has been waiting for you to claim for a very long time.

Hatred has been holding me back for years, but **forgiving** and **letting it go** has healed me and it was actually my **key to success** and everything else. Now if you start forgiving from now onwards without even hearing an apology, you will be healing yourself and you'll start to be successful in the other things you are pursuing in life. Trust me on this one; forgiving has really helped to achieve everything that I have today.

Now let's take a look, if you are holding a hot coal in your hand and waiting to throw it back to the person who has hurt you before, who does get burned by the hot coal while holding it and waiting to throw it back or revenge? Of course it's you. Just forgive and let go so you can heal yourself and your life. You must clear the path of hatred and create a path for love in order to be successful. Nothing can be done without forgiving and love.

I know it's hard, but if you don't start to forgive yourself and the people who had hurt you over the years, you will always hold yourself back and also burn yourself. By forgiving you are not helping the person who has hurt you, but you are helping and healing yourself.

You might think that you are at peace right now or maybe you think that there is nothing or nobody to forgive. On the contrary you need to think back and think hard. You'll find it painful or even crying when you think about what that person or people have done to you. But that's just the only way it can be done.

If you don't feel the pain that means it's not working. If you feel pain and hurt when you think about it, you are doing it right. You should feel the pain, and after that pain you need to release and let go of the pain you have been holding. You will feel relieved afterwards and you will feel happiness and joy you have never even felt before. Your body will feel lighter after releasing the burden you were carrying with you everywhere you went too.

Forgiving alone, can do wonders for you. Try it, you have nothing to lose after all, and you'll see an amazing outcome. I tried it and it worked for me, and you too should try it because it will work for you. "Your sins are the roadblock between **you** and **your** God. That's why He doesn't answer your prayers (Isaiah 59:2)."

Chapter 6
DO SOMETHING ABOUT YOUR LIFE

Let's take a look at the word ignorant. This is the word that mankind have a major challenge with and we underrate it and don't see the importance of it. Now an ignorant person is a person who lacks knowledge and that person is uneducated about that certain topic or life in general.

Yet again, if you are ignorant, poverty becomes your best friend. How can human beings overcome poverty? If we stand together and not against each other, we can easily overcome poverty. I strongly believe that there is plenty of everything in the world for everyone.

If we love God and serve people according to His will, everything will add up and the world will get a positive answer, just like it supposed too. We would live life just like God intended mankind to live on this earth; as one.

It's wise to ask a person who has been there because that person knows better about that particular journey of yours. If you want to travel to Dubai, it would be better that you ask a person who has been to Dubai because he knows more than you, and don't be ignorant.

If you don't have knowledge and experience on something, you are regarded as an ignorant person and that is something you should change from now onwards. Do your own calculations with the information that I have made it available, and see how everything has been there and done while you were not aware.

You have nothing to lose after all. Use your mind, your voice and put some action on whatever you wish to try and you will be amazed of the outcome. Don't be ignorant, just do it now. You must also know that I use the same principles that I am telling you now, and if I am successful using these principles, you can also be successful. You have nothing to lose, the only thing you should do is to try, and only success will be coming your way. Failure is not even an option, but abundance of success and wealth is waiting for you to take the first step.

Invest in yourself. This is a very important thing to do within you. When you are investing on something, you invest so that you will get a profit at the end of a certain period. So it is wise to invest in a correct way so you can get high profits. Same goes for all of us; in everything that we do we are investing for the future ahead.

By sitting down and do nothing about your life, you invest in nothing for the future. In twenty years to come, you will still have nothing because you didn't invest anything while you still had a chance to invest. Ecclesiastes 4:5 tells us that stupid people will fold their hands and watch other people succeed, while they starve themselves to death.

Now this is not what we want at the end of the day. Before you can even invest or help someone, you need to invest and help yourself first, so you can help other people and the whole community, including your friends and family. Service yourself first, before you can service someone else.

If you look at it, how can you help someone while you need help yourself? Help yourself first before you can offer the best service to the next person. Don't be a fool and starve yourself to death. Think about your loved ones, your parents, your kids and anybody you can help financially when you have accumulated enough wealth for yourself.

Think about how happy they will be after helping them with all their needs. Think about the love they will give you each time they see you. These people will admire you and they will be happy because of you. God will be happy because you have served Him through His people.

I'm sure you will also be happy to see your loved ones happy. Being happy is the best feeling ever and everybody needs to be happy. This is one of the other ways to be happy and it is so simple don't you think?

Now don't be a fool as the scripture's tells you and watch other people succeed while you starve to death. Get up and do something about your life. This is your own life and nobody else lives in your life except for yourself. Nobody can think for you or can see what you thinking about except yourself. You are the thinking device and you need to start using your mind and think.

It's the only way to create your future and your desires. Put your energies and focus in the right path and enjoy your life while everything comes to you easily. I'm not saying be jealous of someone else's success, but you should tell your mind that if he could do it, I can also do it.

In this way you push your mind to the highest level. Remember that the mind does everything you think about and you are the only remote control to your mind and future. Again I repeat, invest in yourself now, not in the afternoon, not tomorrow, not next week, but invest in yourself now and I promise you won't be disappointed with the results and outcome of your good investment.

Then one would ask that how can I invest and move forward with my life while I have a lot of problems from my past which I am still dealing with till today? The answer is simple; Isaiah 43:18 tells us that it is vital for us not to dwell on our past. Everyone has a past and we wouldn't move forward if we dwell on our past.

Your past is your passport to success. God allowed everything to happen to you because He wanted to use you so you can testify. After the test, you can only be stronger and God wants the people who have been tested and came out strong so they will warn the rest not to go down that same route or assist them on the pain they are still going through. You should forget and don't think about everything in your past. Your past can never help you in future, but you can learn from it so you can be a better person tomorrow.

God made our eyes in the front of our bodies and on top because it is better to look ahead of you and not to dwell on the things in your past. But learn from them and keep on moving ahead towards your future. So whenever you start to invest on yourself, you shouldn't invest on your broken mistakes you did before, but after you have learned from your mistakes, you will be a better investor.

Look at how successful the people from the other countries are. I'm talking about the people who came to live in South Africa due to diplomatic services. Let's look at this in a positive way. The same people left their countries to do business in South Africa because they know what they want to achieve.

I respect these kind of people so much because they are doing something about their lives and they don't want to starve to death like fools. They left their families, houses, cars and everything else in their countries and they came to South Africa because they saw an opportunity to make some money for their families.

They travelled all the way to our country because they have a vision and they know where they are heading in life. I understand that some of our foreign brothers came to do crime in South Africa, but not all of them are taking part in criminal activities. Then you'll find some of my South African brothers fighting and complain with our foreign brothers because they believe that these people came to steal South African jobs away from them.

The people who think this way are the lazy people who fold their arms and watch other people succeed. By fighting and stealing from our foreign brothers it won't make you wealthy and successful. Stealing from these people's shops can only provide you for one day, and what will you do tomorrow? Stealing from a successful person won't make you successful, but it can provide you for one day or a very short time. You can never steal somebody's success and that means you will still remain the same if you don't do anything about your life. Success comes from within you and not from the outside. Stealing won't change your life, but it will create unpleasant things to come looking for you.

We all have enough of everything in the world and the only thing you should do is to get up and play your part. In fact there are lot of things you can learn from our foreign brothers. They are the people who know what they want in life and they are going for it no matter where and how far it is.

These are the people who take action and they don't just sit around and wait for hand outs, but they take necessary actions to accomplish their goals. Exodus 22:21 tells us clearly that we should not treat our foreign brothers badly when they live with us in our country.

But what we can do is learn a thing or two from them and be successful. It's your own life after all and you need to get up from where you are and do something. Being in other people's issues won't help you at all, except that it will be wasting your precious time that can never be replaced. The time you have, should be invested on yourself so you can be a better person than before and be helpful to your community when you reap and enjoy your profits.

Luke 8:10 clearly tells us that some people have eyes, yet they are blind, they have ears, but yet they are deaf. This takes me back to the word ignorant I have been telling you about. Some people are ignorant and they just don't want to invest in themselves.

With the information I have stated above; please use it and don't be like the people who sit and do nothing about their lives and expect hand outs. From now onwards you are not ignorant and you invest in yourself first. Then Luke 8:10 will be the other way around when it comes to you. You'll have eyes and you'll be wiser; you'll have ears and you'll understand everything.

As Galatians 6:1 tells us that we are Spirits; that means you should see with your spiritual eyes and hear with your spiritual ears. Seeing is not about vision itself, but about the lessons life wants to teach us, and it's all up to you to see them. Not your neighbour neither your friend, but it's up to you to see them.

You are the only person who does the thinking in your mind; you are the only person who does the hearing with your ears and you are also the only person who does the looking with your eyes and not somebody else. Hearing something is another thing and understanding it is something else. Be wise and know the difference.

I remember when I was once a criminal, before the incident that took me to prison. I had a lot of courage to perform the criminal activities that I was part off. And even when I got to prison for something else, my fellow inmates who did robbery and who stole cars for a living talked a lot about the courage.

We did all these kind of crimes because we wanted a better lifestyle to live. We wanted to get out from our current situation to better our lifestyles. We invested in ourselves, but we did it the wrong way which led most of us to be in prison.

Now I want you to put your energies in the right place and invest on yourself in a positive way. Now remember that it's up to you to invest in whatever way you wish to invest, but the criminal root is very risky and it is not even an option.

You could die or go to prison and waste your whole life there, which I'm sure that is not what you would love. But I want you to invest and put your energies in the right place where you won't risk going to prison or killing yourself. This way is the best way to go and it works perfectly.

As I said before, failure is not even an option, but abundance of success and wealth is coming your way. Now I want us to take a look at the **courage** that I had when I did all these sorts of crimes. I had the ability to control fear and I didn't care about the police, going to prison or being dead.

My mind was already fixed on what I wanted and I had no other option unless to go for what I wanted so I could get out of my current standard of living to the next higher level. I made an effort so I could get what I wanted. I used my mental and physical energy to make an attempt and do my best so I could be a better person from who I was yesterday. I was brave and nothing could change my mind on what I was thinking and planning to do. I had confidence in myself and what I thought it was best to do.

Let's make an example of the movie which is acted by Will Smith. Its title is, "The pursuit of happiness". This movie is based on a true story on a man called Chris Gardner who is today a philanthropist and a multimillionaire. If you know the movie you will relate to this story. Now in this movie Will Smith had challenges in finding customers for what he was selling. His relationship with his woman was not good at all and they ended up being on separation because of money issues. He couldn't take care of his family because he didn't have enough money to do so, but he kept on pushing. Then he met a guy who was a stock broker and he loved that job. He wanted to get out from his current standard of living to a better one so he could provide for his family.

There was quite a few of them who also applied for the internship and they all wanted to work in this company, but after six months of training and proving yourself, only one of them was going to get the job.

During those six months Will Smith didn't have time to waste. He used his break time to try and do more work, because he knew that he has fewer hours to work. Since he has to fetch his son at school and go to look for a place to sleep for both of them, yet they didn't have a home anymore. They were chased out by his landlord because he failed to pay the rent money.

But through his effort, he put his mental and physical energy and made an attempt and he made sure that he does his best. He had a vision and a goal and he invested all the time he could get on this one goal that he had and he pushed to be the best because he knew that he didn't have any other option.

Now this is the right way to do things so they can work for you. Don't put your energies in the wrong places where you make yourself strong and happy through someone else's happiness and weakness, because that won't be a solid foundation.

Be like Will Smith, push and push harder till you get it right so you will enjoy your money to the fullest. Control your fear and know that you can do it no matter what comes your way. Be brave in every challenge that comes your way. Make sure that you have confidence in your abilities and push for the best. With this mentality you can never fail, but you are already a winner. Give it your best whenever and in whatever you work on. If you are "down the line/at the bottom" work harder and let your work promotes you to a higher position.

Now let me tell you something about life. Life also has **four seasons** just like the seasons of the year: spring, summer, autumn and winter. Now let me explain to you how these four seasons operate just according to your life:-

SUMMER: - This is the warmest season of the year, when you'd prefer to go to the beach and relax in the sun during your holidays. It is the season when everything is going well in your life and you enjoy life to the fullest. This is the time when you are happy and everything goes well in your life; when you have money and time to spend. It is when everything is going smoothly and you are comfortable about everything you have or have equipped yourself with.

WINTER: - Now this is the coldest season of the year; when you are uncomfortable and you just want the season to quickly get over and done with so you could enjoy your freedom. This season usually comes with heavy snow falls, which makes you stay indoors and don't want to come out at all. It will make you want to stay in bed for the whole day and cause you to be absent from work. You will end up making false report about sick leave by consulting your doctor even when you are not sick; just to get a doctors sick note for work or school. I see you smiling because you know what I'm talking about. This is a wintry, unpleasant and a very unfriendly season for you. It is the time when you can't go to the beach like you used to, because you'll get sick. This is the time when you don't have money for food or to pay for your bills. This is the time when you're in trouble and the people who you thought are your friends will run away from you. It's the time where you'll feel lonely and isolated, where you'll find yourself thinking about what to do next because your friends and relatives have deserted you and you have nobody to rely on in the situation you are facing.

Now I have been through this situation and I know that you also have been through it or you are still facing it. It's a season when you just miss summer and you hope it was here and didn't even leave you in the first place. This season is here to train you in order for you not to slumber and sleep. It is a time where God will just intervene in your life and show you the correct direction to take. This is the season which will make you wiser and fill you with wisdom. This is the season when you'll know who really cares about you. This is the season where you'll see your true friends and what people think off you. This is a very important season where you need to be strong and make sure you don't fall. But most importantly this is a season that will pass very soon, and you just have to take everything that this season will teach you or have taught you so you can use those things in the next seasons to come. This is the season that will make you think hard and you'll want and also plan to transform.

AUTUMN: - Now this is a season where the leaves of some deciduous trees will turn red and gold. This is the season where transformation takes place. Through the challenges that you faced in winter, this is the season where you should really change. The pain that you felt in winter should transform you and get an incentive from the pain you felt. It would be foolish if you don't get any reward from the pain or what has happened to you. You just need to get something out of the pain you felt. Since you felt pain, you need to get something out of it, because there is really a lot you can get out of the pain you felt. This is the time where you need to change if you know what's best for you. Winter was cold and painful for you, but now you need to release this pain and change for the best you could ever possibly be.

SPRING: - Now this is the season when you truly see if the transformation was really applied well. This is a season where you'll see the magnificent display of the flowers in Namaqualand. Everything is glowing and shining. This is the season where you should really feel joy in your heart and be extremely happy. This is the season where you should be full of the joy of spring. This is the season where you need to jump, kick start and move higher. You need to become active and originate. This is the season where you need to rise from the pain you felt in winter and let everybody see the transformation that took place in autumn. This is the season where you need to produce real big and fresh fruits. This is the season where you need to show everybody the real new you; show us that a good change has been done. You need to be glowing, as most woman say. Glow and shine to the world. Be like the flowers in Namaqualand; be who you really want to be, and just fly high up in the sky. Be untouchable and a great example. Be a person who everyone wants to be associated with. Show that you are bigger than your challenges and nothing can ever bring you down. Shine and shine like a star. Live your life like it should be.

But all in all, you have created negative things for yourself with an unconscious mind. But now that you aware of everything, you need to create positive things with a conscious mind. You can now stop the winter season to come to you. You can only stay in the spring and summer season where you'll be living the life you have always desired. You are the creator of your own life, and you can just create these two seasons for yourself and live amongst them; the choice is yours after all.

Here is another example of exercise routine for your whole parts of **the body**:-

LEGS: The legs should be given its own day when you're at the gym. You need to do squats and work with the legs. I know some people just hate the squats and they decide not to give time to the legs and that becomes a problem in the long run because the legs need its attention as well.

ARMS: The arms also need to be worked out during your gym session; including your chest so that everything could balance.

STOMACH: Now this is one of the important parts as well, that most people fail to control. Every person I have met in my life have always wanted to be in control of their stomach, but it gets out of hand through the things they eat and failing to do the exercises as it also needs attention. Most men will tell you that they want to have a six pack, but no action has been taken. I was also one of the men who wanted to have a six pack, but I worked hard for it. I eventually got it after working hard and going an extra mile. It's not sexy at all to see a man with nice legs and arms with a huge stomach. I used to even laugh at the big stomachs as some of my friends still have. Now it's important to work this part as well.

HEAD: Now the head cannot pick up weights, but it also need to be balanced with the rest of the body. Now how do you do that if you can't pick up the weights with your head? You load your mind with knowledge and information. I personally love a woman with a beautiful body, but if I do have a conversation with her and I find that she is a negative person who lacks knowledge and she's just ignorant; I lack interest on her. The mind controls everything and if this woman doesn't have brains, how could I even make her my wife? I can't have a woman whom I cannot relate with. When I talk to you, you need to be on the same level as me, and relate to the things I'm saying. Same goes for women; they love an intelligent man who can use his brain very well and a problem solver. Now even when you have an amazing body, but if you don't have brains to think, you're the same as a person who has a body which is not taken care off. You can also be wise, but if you have a terrible body; it just doesn't add up. You need to balance your body and everything else in your life, end of story.

Each of these parts should be given its own special treatment. Everything needs to balance. In accounting it is shown how important it is to balance the accounts and same goes for your body. Have you noticed how the people who pick up weights look? Have you noticed the ones that focus on the upper body only how do they look? They are bigger at the top and smaller at the bottom.

Now that shouldn't be the case when it comes to everything I have mentioned. It's very important to balance everything in your life and same goes for your body. You need to have time for your kids, time for your wife, time to work, time for friends and time for fun. If something is left out or gets a small portion of your time, than you'll have a problem. You need to balance your life real well so everything will look and feel good for yourself.

Let me close off with four very important factors of life, namely the **intellectual; social; physical** and **spiritual.** Take note that these will always go together and they must always be balanced to enjoy a good and comfortable life.

INTELLECTUAL: This is the reasoning power of the mind and the ability to think rationally. You must be somebody who enjoys doing mental activities that will keep you thinking at all times. Thinking is good, but thinking about good things is the best. You create your life by the way you think and what you are thinking about is something that you'll get in future. You must be someone who has a highly developed knowledge of what you thinking about and creating.

Ecclesiastes 7:11-12 tells us that when you have wisdom you are far better than a person who has inheritance. I'm sure you know someone or a few people who have once inherited something from their parents, more; especially when it comes to money.

It's quite a few of them who have made profits from the inheritance they have got from the parents. But mostly they finish the lump sum in a very short period of time. Why is that so? It's because these kinds of people don't have wisdom at all. They got the money, but they didn't know how to use the money because there is no wisdom in their heads; and that's why this verse is telling you that wisdom is better than inheritance. Wisdom will protect you just like the money would do, but knowledge will lead you to the best life you can ever live. You need to be equipped with knowledge so you can face life and handle it well.

When you follow what have been taught to you and meditate on it, you will live a peaceful life and not be like the ones that are dead. Get wisdom and understanding so you will remember and do as you are told. If you are really wise, don't reject wisdom because she will watch over you at all times. She will be leading you whenever you think and she will always be there.

Wisdom is the principal and therefore she should be part of your life if you wish to achieve all your desires. She comes with grate help and understanding. When you have wisdom, you have everything. When you're wise enough and cherish the wisdom that you have, all that you desire will come looking for you. With wisdom in your life, she will give you the crown to be her King and rule over everything on earth just like God created you to do (Proverbs 4:4-9).

If you're truly wise, wisdom will assist you to obtain what you desire, and when you live as a good person, your knowledge will assist further in getting all your wishes (Proverbs 9:10). It's far better to be wise than to be rich, because if you are wise and lose everything that you possess, you can still get all that you have lost, and even more.; just like Job, the man of God (Proverbs 16:16). And lastly, if you are clever and wise, you will want to learn and equip yourself with new things and knowledge (Proverbs 18:15).

SOCIAL: This is where you should pursue in living in an organized community. We should strive in learning to live with other people. You should bring a complete change in the society you are living in, and be helpful at all times. And always promote companionship. As most people do, they tend to focus on giving love to their loved ones only that is family and friends.

This is all important when put together with the love you give your kids, parents, friends and relatives. Micah 4:6, God said, I will gather my people; and that's why we should stay united.

All relationships are very important and they need to be taken care off and allowed to grow. I personally don't have a father and mother; yet again I also have a broken relationship with my siblings. Both my brother and sister were born outside my parent's marriage and I never got to have a relationship with them as I was going up. I didn't live with them and I didn't have anybody to turn to when things went bad in life. I needed someone who can guide me, give advice and support me. Some of the people I knew would talk about the bond they have with their older sister or brother, but I never got to relate to that because my siblings are still absent in my life. They would show me clothes and shoes that their siblings had bought them, but I couldn't relate to that either. In fact, it made me hate my father more for not supporting me as he should have, and I also hated and didn't want anything to do with my siblings because they have never worried themselves with me as their small brother.

They have never even bought a t-shirt or a pair of socks for me and they left me to face the world alone even though they knew how my father was. I didn't even get support financially or in any form from them when I needed them the most. They have never even come once to visit me in prison, even though they know that I am in prison. Not that I want money or needed a visit from them, but to show that they are concerned about me. I am supporting myself and I need nothing from them. The only thing they could have done is to show that we share the same blood and support me through the hardship I am going through. But in fact I get support from other people who are not even my family. I then came to realise that the real family you could ever have, is not basically your own blood family, but the people who love you and show support to you at all times. And therefore I thank

131

the people who have been with me even though I wasn't the best person they could be around with.

I don't even know my sisters kids and I was not even present the time she was getting married. It's not because we had a fight before, but because of something I don't even understand myself. What I know is, we have a broken relationship. I also have three girls now and our kids have never seen each other. The last time I even saw my siblings was the time when we buried our father and that was the last time I saw them.

But through my healing, I know that I have a challenge to reunite myself with my siblings together with our children. I came to realise that it is not about me only, but also our kids. As much as I didn't get a brother and sister's love, I would love to see my kids being helpful to each other. I came to realise that when you are sick sleeping in your bed or in hospital and you are about to die. You need people you love and have relationships with, not your money, cars and qualifications. Have you ever seen or heard a person who is dying in bed asking for his millions; asking them to bring 10 million so he could see it since he wants to look at the money for the last time before he dies? That has never happened. People need people around them when they about to die. They ask to see a certain somebody and that person is called to say his/her goodbyes.

I came to a decision that I should follow and make things right. I made a decision to fix all my relationships and make them grow and work for all of us. I am not the only one who has a task to fix what's broken. There are a lot of people who are just like me, and they need to start working on their relationships.

Maybe you are one of the people I'm talking about, but I'm here to tell you that it's never too late to fix what's broken. It might not be easy through what has happened, but the fact that you are still alive that mean you can still fix everything. If it's broken, it can be fixed. If there is love, it can be done. Imagine reuniting after so many years of hatred. Can you imagine the joy you would feel in your life? It would be like there was a gap in your life that needed to be filled, but the truth is, there was a gap and you filled it up. It shows that you have played your part in this world and you deserve a reward for that. You must release the anger and pain you feel deep down in your heart and let it go. This healing process will bring better things to you, but by holding back, you are closing your door of success. Let us hold hands and fix what we broke with our own hands and words.

Physical: Now this is the part where you need to show your super natural features; your body. Remember that God lives inside your body and you must make sure you take good care of your whole body. That body should be respected and taken good care of because it is God's temple.

Is God really important to you? If your answer is yes, that means you should take good care of the place He lives in. Just like your house or home. You live inside the house, but you have to make sure that the outside of the house is looking super good at all times. If you don't look after it, bad things that are not needed are being invited and welcomed. If the whole yard is not looking good and taken good care off, the snakes will come for a visit; and the same thing applies when it comes to your body. If you don't look and take good care of it, your body will look weird and you will feel uncomfortable with your own body. You will invite and welcome all kind of diseases into your life, just by not taking good care of your body. If you really love God, you should make sure that He lives in a very decent place. You can't be making your home yard clean so you can live peaceful in your house, and forget about the yard that God lives in; your body. This things work in a same way; look after your body, as you look after your yard.

First thing that shows that you don't love your body. Proverbs 20:1, it's not wise to be drunk. When you are drunk you act like a fool and get into unnecessary fights. Secondly; Proverbs 23:1-3, When you have been invited to celebrate and eat with your friends, relatives or neighbour, use your best manners when you eat and respect yourself. Don't try to finish all the food because you will be killing yourself. Don't be greedy because you see all the nice and tasty food, because it might not be good for your health.

This is an interesting topic, let me just continue. Proverbs 23:20-21, don't drink or eat too much, because these two things will make you poor. 1Timothy 4:8, exercise is always good for your body because it also prolongs your life and make you look young, feel good and fresh.

And lastly, you should be very strong in the body, as you are in your Spirit (3 John 2). If you are only strong in the Spirit and not your body, this means that you are failing to balance your life well and that is a challenge. You need to balance every aspect in your life, and that will help you in future.

Spiritual: Now this is your soul we're talking about here. Now what is a Spirit? The Spirit is the power that you have within you right now and you are called as a supernatural being. God lives in you and He is the Spirit, as I have shown you using the scriptures.

Now, to make sure that you draw all the success and wealth that you need, you have to understand that you are a supernatural being and you're truly a spirit being that lives within the body. 99% of who you are is the spirit and the other 1% is body. You create everything with the spirit that lies within and you can achieve all your desires within a specific space of time when you believe you could achieve those things. The spirit helps you in everything that you want to achieve, and nothing is done without the spirit. In my next book that I'm currently busy with, I will go in deep on this topic of the spirit.

Now let us go to the next point. You should always know that your trials and tribulations (challenges) are like a soccer team. In order for you to go to the next stage in life, you need to be tested first so you can qualify for the next stage. The hardship you experience during your test will determine whether you're ready for the next stage. But the thing that will really take you to the next stage is the action you take during your experience.

A soccer team cannot just go to the world cup or the African Cup of Nations without qualifying to that stage. A soccer team won't just win the world cup without qualifying to be in the tournament first. They have to play and fight for a position in the tournament. Same thing applies to your life. When challenges come towards you, just know that they are not only just challenges, but they are promotions that came to take you to the next stage in your life. With the action that you take, you could be promoted. Since you already in that challenge, it shows that you're ready to go to the next stage in life. But the thing that will really take you to the next stage is the action that you take during your challenges. You have to win and overcome that challenge so you can go to the next stage in your life. Your challenge is just a promotion to take you to the next level in your life.

The truth is, if I didn't go to prison I wouldn't be where I am today. Maybe I would still be stuck on alcohol and drugs. But after I went to prison I found myself and I knew that God really exists since He has always been with me through everything I have been through. I can go on and on about this topic, but the fact still remains, that if I didn't go to prison, you wouldn't be reading this book right now. Going to prison was a challenge to me, but the actions and decisions I took throughout my challenge put me where I am today and made me the man I am today.

When you're lonely, it's a good time to work on yourself. Put on the sign that you always see on hotel rooms, (**Please Do Not Disturb**). You don't need any interruptions, just work on yourself first. You should upgrade yourself first, before you could upgrade people or people's life. You'll only help people with something you know or have.

If you tried something and it didn't work for you, change your focus. I also had my focus on things that didn't help me, but soon after I changed my focus, I saw a huge change in my life and my focus brought me to where I am today.

And when you have shifted your focus to something that you love to do, stick to that plan and don't keep changing your mind because you won't achieve anything if you keep changing and not sure what you want or need. Whatever you start, you must finish it. You must always stay focus. I've also been there; I was not sure of what I wanted and I kept on changing my plans, and that's what really made me not to achieve what I was pursuing all this time.

Connect with the inner man within you. Work together with him, listen to him when he speaks, and follow his lead. This is the way that will make you achieve your goals in the quickest way. Don't rely on yourself and think the power comes from the body, but rely on the inner man who lies within you, because all power comes from him.

Tell yourself that whether you go around it, whether you go over it, whether you go under it and weather you go through it, I'm going to make it. Whatever you are pursing, nothing will ever stop you from achieving it. Tell yourself that you have to make it to the other side dark or blue. If you go with this statement, nothing can overcome your abilities and powers that lies within you right now.

When you accept God and this truth I'm telling you. You'll start to see things in a different way. You'll see things in a spiritual eye and you'll know that you're already rich. The only thing you have to do is to put that mental money on your hand with some actions you need to take so it will become physical money to you. With that, you can do everything you have ever desired or wished to do. Like buying a new luxury car, a new big house, spoil your loved ones, travel the world, be admired and loved by everyone, and not just exists, but to live life to the fullest.

It's true that the minute you get rich and obtain a lot of money, every good thing will come looking for you. Everyone wants to take part in your life, even celebrities will want to be around you. People you once looked up too, and now they will be the ones who want to be around you and take part in your life. You will also be celebrated and you will be living your dream life. The secret behind all this is to put the money that you already possess in your head to your hands.

This book is like a recipe book when you want to do your baking. And to make good tasting cakes, you need to follow all the ingredients that I have included in this recipe book. When you follow this recipe book accordingly when you're baking, not your cakes this time, but your future that is ahead of you; you will find life much easier than before and everything will turn out well on your side.

You will enjoy the future you have baked for yourself through the ingredients I have listed and given you. The only thing that is left for you to do is to mix everything together and put it into action, your oven.

Wouldn't you love it when your future that you have baked comes out perfectly, smelling good and very tasty? I'm sure you would love that. The thing you have to do is to follow these easy steps on this recipe book so you will enjoy a very happy and a satisfying life.

Your life should be like a cricket match. Every time you go in to bat you should make a difference and score as many runs as possible for your team. As you were born, you came to this world to make a difference, and by the performance you put during your life can make you score so many points and runs into your life. That is the aim after all, to get in the field and make a difference by serving your team well and scoring as many points as you can.

Same applies in your life; you already in the field just by being here on earth and you need to make a difference by scoring as many points for yourself and to serve God. Don't get into the cricket field and come out with a big duck, zero points you made; a liability to your team that was looking forward for the change you were supposed to deliver and come with, but you end up failing.

Again, the same rule applies in your life, your parents and the people around are looking forward for the change you came to deliver and bring into this world, and you should deliver to your fullest ability as expected too.

Since you have been given a chance and an opportunity by being in this world to alter and put on your best performance, you must use this chance to your fullest capabilities. You must not go out with a duck, dying without anything in your bank account for your children, and no difference was made by you. Yet you got an opportunity to be somebody or something big in life, something you have always wished to be.

Do you enjoy keeping on praising other people for their success? What about your own success? Don't you wish to be there as well? Don't you wish to be praised as well? Don't you wish to be admired by everyone? Don't you wish to have everything that your role model has and even more; Don't you wish to be greater than the people you look up too?

Let me tell you that everything is in your own power right now as I speak to you. Yes I said it, **everything is within you**. You can make a change now and today by making your dreams come towards you and turning them into a reality. So why wait? Start now!

The reason why you'll find people angry, frustrated and talk nasty things about other people it's because they are lonely, isolated and miserable. They isolate themselves from their own world and life. You need to connect with

God inside you so you won't feel lonely, isolated and miserable.

You'll find life easier and you'll find a person to communicate with at any time of the day. He won't complain about anything but He will always be with you. You need to communicate with the voice inside you. You need to communicate with the greatness that lies within you. And you need to communicate with God inside you so you won't ever be isolated and you'll be able to have inner peace, which will lead to your outside world to prosper, since you already done the inner part and connected with God. When you work with God everything you touch becomes a success.

God has allowed us to rule everything our own hands have made, and He made sure that He put everything under our control and the power we possess inside us (Psalms 8:6). He then informs us that if we listen to Him as He speaks, we will be secured in everything we touch (Proverbs 1:33).

God also didn't just leave us to pursue life on our own. He came to live in us and also gave us guidance. He also tells you that you should know where you are going, because if you don't, you will get lost (Proverbs 4:26).

He continues to tell you that if you want to live a good life and enjoy it to your fullest, stop being a fool and being ignorant. But learn to hear and understand Him as He shows you the way to real life and as He speaks (Proverbs 9:6)

If you only talk one way and you don't listen to Him, you will destroy yourself by being ignorant and arrogant. But if you are wise enough, you will listen and respect His teachings (Proverbs 10:8). If you don't listen to what I'm telling you throughout this book, you will not acquire what you desire and you will feel sorry for yourself all your life. When your desires all come true through listening and doing as instructed, you will be the happiest person on earth. You would have mastered what is expected from you and you will live a comfortable life forever. Now isn't that what you what and desire?

I'm sure it is; everybody would love that. You will be like a tree which is along the river and you will be producing big fresh fruits every time (Proverbs 13:12). But when you reject God who is inside you right now, you will reap what you have sowed and you will be destroyed. And if you respect His teachings, you will get an incentive for what you have done (Proverbs 13:13).

Now I'm giving you a real life because I need everyone to up his/her game, no matter what is your current situation right now. Just by reading and applying this book to your life, you can prolong your life and you could reach 100 years and above. Remember that you are the creator of your life, and you can make yourself reach 100 years and above. Not only that, you can reach those years while you are still fresh and being able to run. It's all in your mind-set and how you carry yourself from now onwards. Show me what you eat mentally and physically and I will tell you how your tomorrow will be.

You must tell yourself that good things are supposed to happen to you every minute of the day, and you'll be shocked of the outcome when you keep repeating this statement. Every step you take counts towards your future, as long as you are going somewhere. One day when you put all of your steps together, you'll be shocked how far you have come too. Everything works for the better and they all keep adding up as pieces of a puzzle in your mind.

When days are dark, don't sit in that darkness and wait for the light that you don't know when it will come. You need to take steps forward in order to see the light. Move forward at all times, even though it might seem hard, but keep moving.

Tomorrow doesn't starts tomorrow, but tomorrow starts today. Do everything that you can do today, holding in mind that you're already in and working for the day ahead of you. Laziness will make you poor, but if you start working for tomorrow today, you will be rich.

I have noticed that most people if not all, want the best for themselves. Even a man who knows he will never get that something or some woman, but deep down in his heart he will love and cherish that woman. Funny don't you think ladies?

We as men will sit and talk about you or the woman on television, about her beauty, and more especially her body. We as men would talk about how much we love that body and so forth, even though we know that we can never win that woman even if we do meet her in person.

We will take no action when it comes to approaching her because we know that she is way out of our league, yet some guys do take chances, shame. I also know that you ladies do talk about us as well, but I won't comment on that one for now, I'll just focus on us men.

The best way to get the woman you desire to marry one day is simple. Just up your game, improve your life once and for all. Simple don't you think? A woman would love to see that she would be secured and taken care off at all times. How can you be her provider if you can't even provide for yourself? Up your game and improve yourself so you can claim and obtain what you need.

I personally would love to meet, have dinner and chat with Nikki Minaj one day. I know that from where I was before, I couldn't have met her. I didn't even have money to buy a plane ticket to go see Nikki or go to one of her shows. But now that I am in control of my life and doing something positive with my life, I do know now that it's highly possible to meet her.

And from controlling my life and taking it to the next level, I could also be blessed enough to meet Gabrielle Union, Taraji P Henson and Melissa Ford. And I would also be honoured to meet Richard Branson and spend at least one weekend at Necker Island with him while gathering more information as I get to know more about him. Therefore, in order to meet these kinds of people, I have to start working with myself and make sure that I am fully improved from what I was yesterday, and that is when the opportunity will present itself.

Do you think the national team goal keeper Itumeleng Kunene would have dated Minenenle Dlamini if he was not earning the millions he earns? Do you think he would have dated her if he earned R5 000 a month? I personally don't think so. Do you think Kanye West would have married Kim K if he didn't have the money he has? Again I personally don't think so and I don't know about you. Yet I'm almost sure you would agree with me.

Don't get me wrong. It's not that these ladies are gold diggers, they are not. They are making their own millions themselves. My point is; there is a level you need to be in, so that you may get what you want. If these men were not in the level they are in, they couldn't have dated these ladies, because these ladies have standards and they couldn't just settle for anything or anyone. They have worked hard to get to where they are today and they had to get men who are going to complete their lives. And you too cannot just settle for anything or anyone if you have standards, because you also want the best for yourself.

When you want to catch someone who is on top of the roof, take a ladder and climb up till you also get to the top of the roof. In that way you will be equally yoked with that person or that something, and that is the way you can get what you have been longing for so many years. Only than when you are on that top level, it is when you'll get anything and everything that you desire. It won't fall down to where you are, but you need to climb up the ladder.

The soccer teams playing in the first division league have their own championship league and they play against each other. There is also a second division league and those teams also play amongst each other. You won't find a team which is playing in the second division league, playing against the other teams in the first division league for their cup games. But you can find a team which was in the second division league the previous year playing in the first division league the following year. How is that possible? The team that worked very hard ended up on the first position, so that it can be promoted to the next highest level. Same principle applies in our lives.

You cannot play in the next highest level or league unless you work hard where you are right now so you could qualify and be where you want to be. If you want to be married to the best wife ever, be the best man you could be first so you could get what you want.

If you want your wife to treat you like a king, you must first treat her like a queen. And if you want your husband to treat you like a queen, you must first treat him like a king. Everything has to start within you first before you can attract anything or anyone into your life. Upgrade yourself first so you could be what you want to be.

But if you don't have money or in a lower level, you'll get things that are in that level you're in. And you'll never get to be in the top level or have a taste of what's on top unless you make a decision and up your game and move on to the next level you can possibly be in.

You get to date and marry anyone in the world and choose from the finest ladies because you have the money. In isiZulu we say, "Indoda iyindoda ngezinkomo zayo". It means that a man is a man with the money that he possesses. I always hear people say money makes the world go round, and this statement is true. All the people I have mentioned didn't settle for less, but they moved along the same level they are in.

I personally wouldn't settle for less and most probably you wouldn't too. Certainly from where you are right now there is a lot of things you want to acquire and achieve, and the only way you can do that is to get up, fight to be in the next level and do something about your life. Surely you want the best in everything; you want the best house, the best cars, and the best husband/wife in your life. Someone who will love, respect, admires and be proud of your achievements.

I'm sure you wouldn't be happy if your partner keeps admiring other people in front of your face, while you're not even close to being in that level of the person that your partner admires. It will be your fault because you didn't do anything about your life while you still had a chance.

No one can push you to do something about your life, unless you decide now that in three months' time I will be in the next level and not where I am today. You can change everything by the decision you'll make now. You can change the way you think in order to get where you need to be, and you must do it now.

It's not over while you're still alive. It's not over while the game is still on and the referee/God hasn't blown his whistle. Even in injury time a team can score three goals and win the game. You should do the same, pick up the pace and pick yourself up now and take necessary actions to accomplish your dreams.

Have you ever wondered how did some American people who were homeless become successful, people like Chris Gardner? How did they make it from nothing to multimillionaires? These people like Chris went through a lot of challenges and hardships, but they never thought of giving up.

They made a choice and decided to convert their pain into a success. When you're already in pain, you need to find an incentive from the discomfort, physical, emotional and mental distress. I personally made bad choices from the past and they brought me pain, but through those hard times I was facing, I made another choice to endure my current situation and better myself.

I told myself that the way I landed myself in the pain, is going to be the same way I pull myself out of it and find an incentive out of the suffering I felt. You can't just get in and come out without anything. Get in, and come out with what's best for you, something that will help you tomorrow.

I converted my pain and got something out of it. At the end of your challenge, there is a promotion waiting for you. For you to receive your promotion, you need to be prepared for it by the choices you'll make from that time.

You need to know that there is no other option but to be successful. There is only plan A and no plan B; and only plan A will take you to your final destination.

Bishop TD Jakes once said, "Run for your dreams; Run after your destiny. And if you once messed up in primary school, you once messed up in high school, and you once messed up in university; but when God gives you a chance for an escape, don't be cute, but run after your destiny, oh God! You better run for your destiny."

I totally agree with Bishop Jakes with everything that he mentions when he talks about running after your dreams. The reason that you bought this book you're reading now means that something is going to happen in your life and you need to pick up the pace.

The fact that you have come to realise these facts that I am informing you about throughout as you're reading, means that you should run for your dreams. You must run faster than before - there is no time to stop, since the time is also running fast and it cannot stop.

Learn from your past and run as fast as you can and make sure you never stop. It's also true that automatically when you run for your dreams, you'll leave all your history behind you and you'll chase what's ahead and in front of you.

You don't get time to try and fix your past. You don't get time to think about the past. You don't get time to regret on what you have done in your past, but you only get time to look ahead and focus on what's in front of you.

That's why it's important for you to start running now; run for your dreams and never look back. Once you start running now, all your focus and energy is ahead of you, on your dreams. Once you look back there is a high possibility for you to trip and fall, but if you continue to look ahead and run towards your dreams, nothing can ever stop you from reaching your goals.

To achieve and not to achieve your goals is entirely up to you. And my advice to you is to run as fast as you can for your dreams, run now and run faster. And make sure that when you fight, you hit the target and don't miss. Do it like Floyd Mayweather JR and hit where your punches will score points for you, so that you'll always be undefeated by your challenges. And make sure you run with a goal in mind in order for yourself to conceive it (1 Corinthians 9:26).

Chapter 7

YOU ARE THE CREATOR OF YOUR OWN LIFE & YOU REAP WHAT YOU SOWED

Now, as much as I wrote this book with a lot of information taken from the Bible, I also wrote it because of my life experiences. I know that everything that I say throughout the book is a fact because it's something I personally went through and experienced over the past years.

Through my journey I was unconscious and I didn't have the information that I have today, and so I created my life with an unconscious mind which eventually cost me to go through the prison walls and stay there for years.

During my term of incarceration I had a lot of time to observe and edit what I didn't want in my life. I came to realise that I was the creator of my own life, including every person and everything around me. My mind became conscious about everything and the way life should be lived.

I saw how ignorant I was before and I was not the only one. So I made a choice and a decision to help and inform everyone who is going to read this book about the challenges we face in life because of our ignorance.

I also didn't want my children to go through the same process I went through and travel the life journey with an unconscious mind. I made a choice to help and change people's mind so you too can have a conscious mind like I do.

In this way everyone, including yourself can enjoy life to the fullest and do, be or have anything you have ever desired in your life. With this book you'll just never go wrong. I'm talking about things that I have already tested in my life and everything came positive.

I was out of control before, but I took control of my life again before it was too late. Now I'm living my dream and my life is so much easier. Therefore, now it's your time to be in control as well and create your life and everything else with a conscious mind.

Just look back into your life. You'll see that you have created the situation you're in right now. It could be your thought about it or you spoke about it previously. If you think back, you'll know that I'm right. And you are the only person who can take yourself out of it. Nobody else except you.

Your whole life you created your future with an unconscious mind and you were unaware that you're creating your future, but from now onwards you will create your future while you're aware and with a conscious mind every step you take. You create your future and everything else. Take note of everything around you and control everything as you move forward and be successful in your journey.

I was once a DJ, but after telling myself that I need my own equipment to be a DJ, I waited for that moment which never came till today. I had already told myself that I can't do it without my own equipment even though I was going to places with one of the biggest DJs at that time.

My dream vanished in front of me because of what I thought about with my negative belief and I created my future. If only I didn't think in this negative way, I would be far in life as a DJ. I created my future with an unconscious mind. Thank God that my mind is conscious today and it's never too late to be and do anything I desire to do. Watch the space because I'm also practising everything that I'm revealing on this book.

Chris Gardner once said, "You need to have plan A and not plan B". And I totally agree with him in this point. But you'll find people telling you that you must always have plan B just in case your plan A fails. I was also told by some people that I must have plan B in everything that I do, but I never took that advice or even recommend for someone to have plan B. Just by doing so, having plan A, B & C, you have already created your plan A to fail. But if you have only plan A you're working with and you put all your energy and effort in it, there is no way that it won't work. Plan A will have no place to run too. It can't run to plan B or plan C because you didn't create or plan for it and so plan A knows that he should work for you and become a success.

If you have watched the Pursuit of Happiness' or read the book itself, you will see that it has been proven in Chris Gardner's life that if you have plan A only it will work for you no matter how challenging it is. He made sure that he pushed with everything that he had to become a stock broker without any qualifications of being a broker. So when Chris said you must have plan A only and not plan B, he is talking about something that has worked for him and a proof to us all that when you give it your best shot in your plan A, surely it will work for you.

The fact that you're reading this book shows clearly that if you only have plan A, it will work for you. During my term of incarceration I was studying Business Management till things went wrong inside prison and I couldn't continue with my business studies, till I decided to start writing a book.

I put all my energies in the book I was writing since I had already planned to write a book at the beginning of my sentence. As I was writing the book my dream became brighter each day, till one day things were back to normal with our studies and I was supposed to continue with my Business studies.

I had already bought text books and I had seen my money wasted, after I couldn't continue with my education. But as soon as I was about to continue after everything was back to normal, I couldn't continue because I was committed to the book I was writing.

154

Then I decided not to waste my time since I already had sleepless night writing this book. And from those days I never looked back and I only had plan A, I was working with. Without even a qualification of being a writer, I knew that I was good in writing and writing is what I wanted to do and I must focus and put everything that I have on writing so I could achieve my dreams.

I spent months of writing this book and it was my only option I had. I didn't have plan B because I knew that plan B was going to cancel my plan A and I won't achieve what I was planning to achieve.

I also have a friend who dropped out of tertiary. Both his parents are graduates and they provide the best education for my friend. His father has graduated so many times and he is a doctor in his field of education. Yet my friend doesn't want anything to do with school and he doesn't want to study any further.

At that moment he was also an underground singer, and he was telling me about his music talent whenever I told him that he shouldn't drop out from school, more especially since his parents a funding his education.

His mother was worried about him and asked me to talk to his son about school, but still he didn't listen to my advice. I even told him that if I had an opportunity like the one he has, I would grab it with both hands since my father couldn't afford to pay any tertiary fees for me after my matric.

My friend told me that he could see where he is going with his music and he is very close in achieving his goal. I just saw it as he was gambling with his life since there was nothing promising in his career, but he was the only one who knew about his dream and also knew where he is going with it.

About two years later he got a recording deal with one of the biggest recording companies in South Africa, and today he is a well-known musician with his own recording company. As much as I was not sure that he was going to be successful or not, he was the only person who knew where he was going too, because he is the only driver and the creator of his life.

Now through these two stories, please don't get me wrong. I'm not saying education is not important or you must drop out of school. What worked for me, might not work for you. And what worked for somebody else, might not work for you either. Maybe your success may come through education. You need to know what **you** want to do, not somebody else; but **you**. My point is, when you have plan B, automatically you cancelling your plan A and creating it not to work for you. And that's why it is important to have plan A and give it your best shot.

It has worked for me and many other people. It means that it is a proven method that will work for you too. Your God sees everything that you do in private, and He will give you an incentive for it in public (Matthew 6:18).

It's very important to control and watch what you eat. I'm not talking about physical food here, but the things that you feed your mind with. Anger, hatred and so forth; all these things will eventually come out one day and they will be out of your control because you are busy loading them now. Remember that, this is what happen to me and I know what I'm talking about. This is the law, whatever you put in you; you will get exactly that in return.

This is the law; you reap what you sow, just like when you are reaping music from a computer. You sow the music you want to reap in the software that you'll use, than you reap the music. By the time you play or listen to the music you had reaped, it will be the same music or songs that you loaded and you'll get what you wanted in the first place.

Same thing happens even here. Whatever you put in, will be taken out some day, and that's why I ask you to meditate on this book because what you will be reading and putting in, will be taken out tomorrow and you be satisfied with the outcome.

I tell you for certain that you cannot fool God. He is in control and you will reap everything that you sow from today (Galatians 6:7). What you insert today will be what you'll be watching tomorrow. It's simple as that; we're all products of our past. What we are today is what we have been loading ourselves in private for years, and what we see now in public is the outcome of what we really are.

If you put in extra, you'll get out something extra for yourself. The harder you work in your mind, the more pleasing results you'll get tomorrow. Everything that you need is inside you right now. There is nothing you'll get from outside, except for that everything is stored inside you as it is.

The only thing you need to do is take what you already have and put it on the outside world so your body can use. Simple; nothing more and nothing less, just do it. Remember in school we were given homework and activities to do? I am also giving you an activity and homework you need to do so you can change and take control of everything around you.

If you pass this test, you'll get a huge reward for it. Pass this activity and you get abundance of wealth and success. Isn't that what you wanted in the first place? You have nothing to lose, just go on and make yourself rich with what you have with you right now.

You have been given everything, but still you don't want to use what you have. Are you happy with your current situation? How long will you be broke and keep asking the people around you for money? How long will the people around you feel sorry for you for being broke?

Don't you think it's high time to be in control and let them ask money from you? Don't you think that it would be a good feeling after all? You would really feel happy deep inside you for helping the people that were helping you for many years. But everything has to start now and within you.

Your God will reward you for everything that you'll do from today (Psalms 62:12). Your God will reward you if you work and go according to His Laws. Everything that you have including yourself will prosper; you will have peace and happiness in your heart that no one could understand except for yourself, and everything in your life will be perfect (Psalms 128:1-2).

You will harvest and eat every action of yours till you become a product of what you have sown (Proverbs 1:31). Don't think that if you sow something in private, you will be rewarded for something else in public. What you put in will definitely be what you'll get out.

Your wicked ways and thoughts will be what you are and that won't help you at all in becoming what you wish to be. But being a good person at all times will draw you closer to the achievements that are waiting for you (Proverbs 10:2).

If you are evil, God won't let you have what you desire, but if you respect God's Laws, you will always be successful (Proverbs 10:3). If you are wicked, everything of yours will perish, but if you are really a good person, you will do the right thing and be successful (Proverbs 11:5). Cruel people destroy themselves with what they think about, but kind people are always rewarded for their work (Proverbs 11:17-19).

Whatever the wicked people fear, will definitely happen to them, but the desires of the good people who listens to the Laws of God that I am providing you, shall be granted (Proverbs 10:24).

Now this is important and you should really take note of this. If you focus on bad and negative things; that is exactly what will happen to you. Whatever you focus on, will definitely take place. Whatever you fear will take control of you and you will be sorry that you focused on fear. **Do not** focus on things that won't help you.

Even when you're in challenges, don't dwell on them, but shift the mind to solutions. And if there is no solution in your matter, **create** one for yourself. Remember that the world was not like this before, some people created everything that you see. So what could stop you to create anything you wish to take place? Nothing can fail you except for yourself; just get up and move.

Life is like this; if two people are given meat to be cooked, and the first one uses water only to cook the meat, while the second person goes an extra mile and she includes salt, onion, potatoes, soup and spices. From your point of view, whose food do you think will taste much better?

Obviously the second person will win because she went an extra mile to make her food taste better. So applies to life as well. We are given everything that we need to make our own perfect lives, the only thing we need to do is to go an extra mile with the thinking and the actions that we take. Just by thinking success, you are already creating a successful life upon yourself.

I once listened to a speech by a former international cricket player Rahul Dravid. He spoke about his journey through cricket from childhood. His father use to go with him to watch cricket as a young boy, till he eventually fell in love with cricket just like his father. As he grew older his school principal was worried about his studies as he was supposed to play cricket during school hours. He got a chance to be on the next level when it comes to cricket, and his father was informed that cricket will stand in his way of studies and he needs to drop playing cricket so he could focus on his studies. But his father's response was that they must do their job and allow him to play cricket, and he will make sure that his school work was up to date, and from there he never looked back. A seed was already planted in him as a small boy and he had to reap what he had sown over the years. He created his own life from childhood as he was thinking only about cricket till he got to the international level.

Floyd Mayweather JR is another perfect example. By the age of seven years he already had his own boxing gloves. And before the age of seven he was already going in and out where boxing was taking place. His father was a boxer, including his uncles; and there was just no way he couldn't be a boxer. As he was surrounded by boxers and boxing equipment from a young age, the seed was already planted deep inside him. And he fell in love with boxing. As he grew older he learnt boxing skills and he thought about boxing and nothing else. I personally understand why he is undefeated and the best in the whole world. The seed was planted long before we even knew him, and the tree is showing now on how well was the seed planted. He created his future with all the energy and focus he invested in, boxing as he was growing up. And the time had to come for him to reap what he had sown.

There are a lot of people who are like these people I have mentioned and if you look at these two you'll notice that both of them didn't have plan B. They focused and invested their energies in what they were doing. They were doing what they **love** on a daily bases and they never thought of giving up through the challenges they faced. This shows that success comes from within and in what you do. You don't have to play a certain type of sport or be a musician or actress to be successful. You just need to invest on yourself, do what you **love** and give it your all and that is when you'll be successful and wealthy beyond measure.

Please don't be like the people who say this was not my year and so I will wait for next year to see what it will bring for me. You must stop expecting people to do things for you. Why don't you do things yourself? It's not about what somebody brings for you, but it's about what do you bring for somebody else; and what do you bring for this world. How can you even say that you are waiting to see what will the New Year bring for you? The New Year doesn't have hands, but you do. Why don't you ask yourself what will you bring for the New Year?

You are the person who has hands and therefore you should be carrying something with you to hand over to the New Year. Just bring a present with you to the New Year and just surprise the year that is ahead of you with the goodies filled in your present that you brought. You are the person who writes your own life with the hands that you have, and the New Year is just a blank piece of paper waiting to be written on. The New Year is always ready for you, and the question is, are you ready for the New Year and what are you going to do with it?

Chapter 8
BE GRATEFUL FOR WHAT YOU HAVE

Gratitude; now this is a very important topic that keeps bringing everything to you. You need to be grateful at all times so you could attract more things into your life. Be grateful for everything you have and everything around you. Stop complaining that you don't have money or anything else. The R1.00 that you have on your hand or your pocket right now, you must be grateful about it.

There is no such thing that you don't have, everyone in the world has something and therefore it's important to start being grateful for whatever or anything that you have. If you appreciate your life and the things that you have, you are creating a path of the things that will appreciate you as well and they will also come looking for you.

Be grateful for waking up in the morning. Be grateful for breathing. Be grateful for the mind that you have, and just be grateful for everything. You know, while I'm still inside the prison walls, I have been grateful for everything around me. I'm sure you might be asking yourself, what is there to be grateful for in prison? But let me tell you that there are many things that you can be grateful for in any situation you in.

As much as money is not allowed in prison, we do use it. You cannot survive anywhere without money, and therefore money plays a major role in people's life. It's even worse in prison, if you don't have money to provide yourself like other prisoners. You will find it very hard inside. The food we eat in prison is terrible, and therefore it is vital for people who have money to buy their own food in prison if ever you can afford it and wish to eat something different or cook it yourself.

Now how is it possible that some prisoners can buy food while in prison? Well, that topic is for another day; what I'm trying to tell you here is how important is to be grateful for what you have wherever you are. Now every time I buy food or receive money, I am grateful for that. When I take out money, I do it with an open heart and I speak with it.

I speak to it and say, "Go to your brothers and sisters and tell them to come and stay with me". And when I receive money, I am grateful for the money I get. I speak to it, showing my appreciation and the love for the money. You know just by doing that, I have never even for once ran out of money. I always have money to buy whatever I wish to buy, only because I am grateful for the money I always give out and receive. Not that I am selling something in prison, but there is always a way that money will come to me.

I also show appreciation for the education I'm getting in prison. I am grateful for just being in prison because of the information and knowledge I am accumulating every day. I am grateful for the prisoners that surrounded me who always give me advice about life and everything else. I am grateful that I am serving few years, while I see other prisoners pulling life sentence in prison. I am grateful that I go to the gym every day and I don't have to pay a cent to keep myself healthy.

I am grateful that God has always been with me throughout my life, since I am still alive and have every part of my body with me. When I think about things I used to do, the fights I used to be in, the car accidents I used to be in, but still I survived everything. And I was grateful for that too. All my life I had been sleeping with different women without a condom and I am grateful that I am still healthy and looking good.

Now this will not sound fascinating to the tax payers, but it's the truth. I am grateful for the free food I get in prison; I am grateful for buying food at a very cheap price than outside; I am grateful for consulting with the doctors for free; I am grateful for the free safety I get from the prison warders; I am grateful for seeing a social worker for free whenever I need to see one; I am grateful for the free education I get; I am grateful for not paying for electricity; I am grateful for not paying for water services; I am grateful for not paying the rates; I am grateful for the bed I sleep in; I am grateful for the free clothes I get; I am grateful for the free toiletries I get; I am even grateful for the people who cook the food for me without payment.

In fact I could go on and on about what I am grateful for in prison because the list is endless and I won't even finish. But I'm naming all these things because I want you to understand that no matter where you are, you can be grateful for **anything**. I'm not implying that there is a good life in prison, I just told you about the advantages of being in prison and I didn't mention the disadvantages.

Some people might not like what I'm saying, but it's the truth. I just want to teach you that you too can be grateful for anything wherever you are. The fact is, in every situation there is an advantage and a disadvantage. In every advantage, there is a disadvantage; and in every disadvantage, there is an advantage, when you look deep into it. And that is what kept me going in prison. I looked only at the advantages and I was grateful for them.

I placed my focus on the advantages and guess what I got out of that, I got more pleasing results. The principle is, whatever you focus on, that's what you are going to get in return. The most precious thing I am grateful for in prison is the **time** I get. I have all the time in the world because there are few things that are surrounding me. The fact is, if I was outside, I wouldn't have got the chance to write this book, and so I used my time I have in a very productive way.

2 Corinthians 2:14, I am grateful that Christ was here to show us the correct way to live life. Don't worry about anything; just be grateful to your God (Philippians 4:6).

God has made me very grateful for everything, and that's why it's easy for me to be grateful for everything in prison; during my hardships (Philippians 4:10). Let me tell you that you too can and should be grateful for everything that you have.

Ephesians 1:16, I never stopped being grateful; even today I still am and I will always be. I'm grateful that you are reading this book, and you too should be grateful that you are reading this book now; because this is the book that will open doors for you, and to everything else.

Maybe you are currently employed and you are not grateful for the job that you have. Before you got the job you are currently in, you wanted the job that you have now. Why are you not grateful about it?

There are people out there who need a job, but you have a job that you are not grateful for. Why don't you just quit the job and open a space for somebody else that needs that job you have? Why waste your time on something that you don't love doing? Is that a wise move? Why do you have to make yourself a slave?

Even if you know that you worth more than what they pay you, but you still settle for less. Why don't you just leave that job and look for something better; something that you deserve? Let me tell you something. You'll always earn less because you are willing to settle for anything just because you need the money. But once you stand up and tell yourself that you know what you worth, and it's something you'll get. You will get what you worth.

168

But the trick and the secret is that you should be grateful for the job that you have, in order for you to get a better one; the one that you deserve; simple as that. Start now and be grateful so you will draw the job that you want closer to you, and obtain it as fast as you appreciate the one that you have.

Again, you are in a relationship or married to a partner that you chose, but you are still not grateful and you looking elsewhere. I didn't choose your partner for you, but you did, but still you not grateful for what you have. You keep looking for better men/women out there yet you don't appreciate what you have. Let me tell you that you won't get a better partner if you don't start to appreciate the one that you have.

You would be dating or married to the most beautiful and loving partner, but still you keep on looking elsewhere as if you will find something better than what you have. Being ungrateful is a terrible sin which breaks a lot of relationships, and you just keep moving back in your life because you are ungrateful of everything around you. You will not go anywhere in life if you continue to be ungrateful. Have the heart of saying thank you for everything that you have, and more things that you will be grateful for will come into your life.

The principle is simple and need to be followed in order to activate and achieve what you desire. What's even the reason for you to look elsewhere while you have someone with you? If you are not happy, why don't you just leave so you could look properly and open a space for someone who will take good care of your partner? What is the need to look for someone while you have someone with you; even worse, you don't appreciate her/him? What would make you appreciate the next one if you are failing to start where you are right now?

Again, gratitude is the key to your success. You won't proceed in life until you start to be grateful for what you have. Be grateful for the relationship that you have. Give it your best and show love to your partner. Don't just say you have failed while you haven't even tried.

Even worse when you're married; there shouldn't be a door that leads you outside. It should be once you in; you are in, and there is no way out. **Work on it** and it will work for you. In prison there are different kinds of gangsters, and one of the rules that they have is, once you in, you are in and there is no way out. When you try to come out after joining their gang, you might even lose your life because the other gang members will come for you.

Same as marriage, once you in, you are in and there should be **no way out**. Didn't you make a promise to God that in sickness and in health, till death do you apart? If you don't keep these words that means you have broken a promise with **your** God and that means you are such a liar. God hates divorce (Malachi 2:16).

What can you really achieve in life if you lie and think you are cheating your God? This has to stop now and you better change. Change your mind-set because you are attracting everything that has ever happened to you and in your relationship. You need to start to be grateful for what you have so you can change the way your partner thinks and act around you.

1 Thessalonians 5:18, for whatever happens in your life, keep thanking God. John 11: 41, I thank you for answering my prayers. Now in this verse Jesus gave thanks to God before his prayer was even answered. He was grateful for waking up Lazarus even before Lazarus was brought to life.

Tell me, how could you say you are walking or you want to be like Christ if you can't even do half of the things he did? You are failing to be grateful, but yet you say you want to be like Christ? You should just stop using Christ name because you know that there are things you're not doing as he did. But if you are willing to change and be like him, you can call Jesus as your brother.

Jesus was grateful before his prayer was answered, and that is how you should approach things. Be grateful and thank God for the millions that you have, even though you don't have them in your physical eyes, but you have them in your spiritual eyes. You need to convert them so they will become a reality.

Be grateful for the R1.00 you can touch, and also be grateful for the millions you see in your mind, so that tomorrow you will touch those million. This is a simple procedure that needs to be followed and applied, in order for you to activate your success and wealth.

Now here is a **thanks giving prayer** that you need to pray daily so you'll bring everything closer to you. I used it and it worked for me. You too can use it because it will work for you:-

I will praise you, Lord!

You saved me from the grave

and kept my enemies

from celebrating my death.

I prayer to you, Lord God,

and you healed me,

saving me from death

and grave.

Your faithful people, Lord,

will praise you with songs

and honour your Holy name.

Your anger lasts a little while,

but your kindness lasts

for a lifetime.

At night we may cry,

but when morning comes

we will celebrate.

I was carefree and thought,

I'll never be shaken!

You, Lord, were my friend,

and you made me strong
as a mighty mountain.
But when you hid your face,
I was crushed.
I prayed to you, Lord,
and in my prayers I said,
What good will it do you
if I am in the grave?
Once I have turned to dust,
How can I praise you
or tell how loyal you are?
Have pity, Lord! Help!
You have turned my sorrows
into joyful dancing.
No longer am I sad
and wearing sackcloth.
I thank you for my heart,
and I will never stop
singing your praises,
my Lord and my God.
(Psalms 30:1-12)

Chapter 9
HOW TO USE FAITH IN ORDER FOR IT TO WORK FOR YOU

To the African people who use African medicine (muthi) would understand what I'm about to say more clearly than anyone else. When a traditional healer gives you muthi to use; he/she will tell you that as you are using the muthi you must speak to it and command it to do whatever purpose you wish for it to do.

Most muthi if not all, requires a person to use his/her voice as he/she commands it to do their plan. This is something that the people who use muthi do, but they don't understand that the true power of what they are doing comes from the inside of them. They take action by using the muthi, then they use the voice and they have faith in the muthi that it will work. Then some people will say that muthi doesn't work and you'll find some people that will tell you that muthi does work perfectly. The secret behind these two statements is that the people who say muthi doesn't work it's because they don't believe in it. And to the people who have used it before and it didn't help them, the problem was because they didn't have faith in the muthi and they doubted it.

Don't get me wrong, I'm not promoting muthi nor criticising it, but I'm trying to clarify something that most African people debate about. Some will say that I have tried muthi before and it didn't work, and some will say I have used muthi from an early age and it's working perfectly.

Then you will find people who will even go to an extent of proving that muthi works perfectly and they start to control things that are happening in the sky, like the lightning and thunder. These kinds of people even go to an extent of fighting through the lightning and thunder till they kill each other. Now the question is; does muthi really work? Now some people won't like this answer, but muthi works perfectly **only if** you **believe** in it.

Again my own father didn't believe in muthi and he lived a very long life with all the sicknesses that he had, and he lived more years than his friends who were using muthi and convinced him to use it as well to prolong his life. But the faith that my father had in God made him survive all the chronic diseases that he had and he was the last person to pass on from his friends.

To the people who say muthi works perfectly and have tried it and it worked, it's because they had so much faith in the muthi from the first place. What really drives the muthi to work is your voice that you use when you are talking and commanding it on what to do, plus the amount of faith that you have within you, and then the action is already taken when the person is using the muthi.

Bear in mind that every living person has some sort of a spirit (the power to perform action) within them. That's why you'll find people who are believers in Christ and some are not, but both these people will be able to perform action. Some are using the spirit that is not pleasing to God and exercising their faith with the bad actions they take. Yet some are using the Spirit of God which is the Holy Spirit by exercising their faith with good actions that is pleasing to God.

I urge you to activate the Holy Spirit that lies within you right now. Jesus Christ was born just like me and you, and he was also here on this earth to show us the way to live a good life. He did miracles with the amount of faith that he had, and you too can also do miracles and even greater things with the amount of faith that you have within you right now as I speak to you.

Now if muthi works only if you have faith in it, that means it cannot work alone and needs you to have faith. Throughout the book I have mentioned that all power comes from the inside, and there is no need for you to use something else to activate the power. Just by having faith and taking necessary actions with your body and nothing else, you can achieve anything you want to achieve.

You don't need to hold something on your hand to activate your power that lies within you. But you only need yourself to have faith in what you want to achieve.

Get that doubt and fear out of your mind because it is Satan who is stopping you to take action. When fear increases, Satan is increasing. But when faith increases, God is increasing as well. Yet again; when fear increases, God decrease, but when faith increases, Satan decrease. All in all, the choice is yours to make. I choose to have faith in everything that I do so that God will increase and He will be with me all the time. He will also take control of your life and He will be the driver if only you allow Him too.

Look at the things Jesus Christ did while he was here on earth. He didn't have any doubt, but he had only faith and he took action and made everything to work for him as he commanded. That's the only thing you also need; have faith and take action. In this way you will make everything work for you and everything you do will become a reality. Go for it and start now. The power that lies within you is so powerful in a way that it can change the whole world, but only if you have faith. Believe in what you are doing and you shall achieve it.

You'll hear that there a prophets who are healing people with a prayed bottle of water, and you'll hear people testifying that they are healed through the water. Now if you look at it, how come they are healed? It's because of the faith they had inside them. Basically those people had healed themselves with believing that they will be healed.

We've heard that Jesus healed people and he said to them, "Your faith has healed you." (Luke 18:42; Matthew

8:13). Hence that he didn't say my faith, but **your** faith is the only power that can make things happen.

Then let's look at a person who was sentenced life imprisonment. How do you think they survive in prison while their whole life is placed in prison? I'm talking about the same people that they were forced to live everything that they had outside, including their wives, kids, family, money, houses and cars.

Some of these people I'm talking about lived the best life outside the prison walls, but they were forced to adapt to the change. Life is not the same as it was outside, but they have to survive. Let me tell you that these people live by faith and they know that one day they will be out. **Faith** is the only thing that keeps them going.

These people have hope and they can see the light in the darkest place. I know these people because I have lived with them. There is absolutely nothing that can move them away from the amount of faith that they have. They will tell you that one day they will be outside in the real world and whatever they had achieved before, they can still achieve when they are given the time and chance. Just look at the amount of faith that these people have.

They just know that one day they will be out and when they do get that chance they can still have everything that they had before, and even more. Hence they're aware that when they come out from prison they will start from scratch.

I personally don't know how I could survive in prison for this long period of time, and I don't know about you. Yet these people who are facing this challenge are surviving quite well inside there. But all of this is being sustained through the faith that they have.

You might think that you don't have that amount of faith within you right now. And I'm telling you that you have even greater faith you possess within you right now. It's just that you don't know and haven't used it. Once you faced with a situation and there is no way out, you will discover the power that you didn't know that you have within you.

You'll know by than that you're strong and powerful only because of the amount of faith that you have. Once you faced and forced into a situation that you never thought you'll be in and there is no way out, you'll activate your true powers that lies within you. Let me inform you that you don't have to be in a tough situation to allow your faith to work for you.

You can activate and use the faith that you possess wherever you are. It's something that you have within you right now. Not something that you have to pay for first before using it. It's free and you don't have to pay a cent for it to be used.

Why do you place little value on things that are so powerful and don't have to pay for? Great things in life are for free and you should realise that now if you were not aware. There are people who are in prison who are multimillionaires, yet you are outside in the real world and you have nothing and **broke**.

You are so broke that you don't even know what you'll eat tomorrow. Yet you have the brain to think with and the faith to achieve what you need. What is really stopping you to be and have what you desire? What makes a person in prison better than you?

Or are you just admitting that he is far better than you? What are you really telling me about yourself, if you say a person with no movement and resources is far better than you? Are you saying that you have failed and you curse the day you were born? You came to this world with nothing and you also want to die with nothing? What example are you showing your kids or your wife/husband?

Do you consider being broke the right way to live? Are you even happy about yourself? If you see no point in living life, why don't you just end your life now and allow other new born babies to come into this world and try to make a change; the same change you are failing to apply? Are you doing the right thing though? This is not the way to live life. Make everything possible with the faith that you have. Everything, and I mean everything is done with faith; you have it, so use it.

2 Corinthians 4:18, the things that are seen don't have much power than the things that are not seen. And that is why you should focus on the things that are not seen because all power comes from them. That's why it was easy for Job to accumulate more wealth after he had lost

everything, because all the power that you need to achieve something comes from within.

There are some people who are living on this earth today who were like Job, people like Donald Trump who were once successful and wealthy, but they lost everything in the long run, but they didn't think of giving up. They accumulated more wealth again and they are successful and wealthy till today. And yet there is someone like you who haven't even tasted success and wealth even once?

Now are you really a good example as you think you are? Do you want to stay like this all your life? Do you want to change your life forever? Are you willing to take a step forward? Apply this book onto your life and achieve everything like great people do. You won't even be like great people on earth, but you will be the greatest.

Ten men with leprosy wanted Jesus to heal them, but one of them was healed. Jesus didn't do anything to all ten men, but he only said go and see the priests. When one man came back to thank Jesus for healing him, Jesus said, **your** faith has healed you (Luke 17:11-19). Again, what healed this man? It was his faith.

Why the other nine men were not healed? It's because they didn't have much faith that they were going to be healed only by Jesus words. It might be that these men thought they would be healed by the priests when they get to them, but that wasn't the case with one of them.

The scriptures tell us clearly that you don't have to use anything to activate your faith so it could work for you.

You don't need to use something that other people tell you to use because all the power comes from within you.

It's also shown throughout the New Testament that even Jesus wasn't the one who was healing the people, but they healed themselves with the faith that they had. These people didn't know that they had the power inside them, but yet we a blessed to know today that all power comes from inside, within you.

We reflect on these people's lives and understand that the power has always been there, it's just that those people didn't know and understand what they have inside them just like you. Now you do know, yet you still don't want to apply the power that you have. You want to sit down, admire and celebrate the lives of the people who are doing something about their lives.

When God said don't worship idols and other gods, He meant that you shouldn't have your faith on something that you can hold, because faith comes from within. And also don't worship other people because you won't have time to worship Him that is living inside you. He wants you to worship Him, the one who is living inside you. You are god and you need to worship yourself with the understanding that God who lives in you is doing everything for you.

So it's true that Jesus came to show us the way to live life. He kept on saying; "You healed yourself" to the people that believed he was healing them. Even today, people still believe in some other people or things that they will or are healing them. Yes these people or things will heal you, only because you have faith that you will be healed; simple as that. I challenge you to heal yourself without going to anybody or using anything to heal yourself. It is possible to heal yourself, I have tried it and it worked.

Luke 18:35-43, Jesus told a man that was blind that he healed himself because of his faith that he had within him. Then I ask you a question, "If you believed that Jesus was here on earth and did all these things, why don't you believe that you can also do these things and heal yourself?"

He has spoken, and he has said you can also do what he did. John 14:12 Jesus said, "I tell you for certain that if you have faith in me, you will do the same things that I am doing. You will do even greater things, now that I am going back to the father."

So what's more could you ask for? Why we don't listen or even try these things and see if they would really work? I have and everything works just like the Bible says. The reason why I even wrote this book it's because I have proven everything that I say on it, and everything works perfectly.

I created for myself to be in prison, and I also created for myself to be where I am today. I created my challenges and when I came to realise that I was the creator, I started to create my own success, and it worked; look at where I am today. So what could stop you as well to achieve everything you desire?

Again in the book of Matthew 8:13 Jesus said, "Your faith has made everything possible" and the man was healed. Luke 8:22-25, it is shown that if fear increases, nothing can be done; but when faith increases everything is made possible. Jesus even asked the disciples if they do have any faith in them. Matthew 8:26, why are you afraid, don't you have any faith in you?

Jesus knew and he was showing us that everything is done by the faith we possess, and nothing is done without faith. Now I'm also asking you if you do have any faith within you since nothing has been done with your life. If you do have faith, why don't you show it that you do? As a believer why don't you prove to yourself that you can do it and make it big in life so you can also help the people who need help?

Matthew 17:17-21, when Jesus disciples failed to heal a child with a demon, he told them that they are very obstinate and they are faithless. Then Jesus spoke to the demon and it went out from the child. Again we see the power of the voice and faith working miracles.

When the disciples asked Jesus on how come they didn't heal the child. Jesus told them that it's because they don't have enough faith and they were faithless. And he makes a promise to them, that if they had faith no bigger than a mustard seed, they could tell a mountain to move from one place to another and it would listen to them.

Take it as Jesus was speaking to you. His disciples were not different from you, and you should apply what Jesus said onto your life. If you could speak and say something;

that same thing can happen. I also did the same thing, I told someone that I was going to take her life away and go to prison for that, and that's what really happened. And this shows that what Jesus had said it is true.

How could I really clarify this point to you so that you will understand it and apply your faith from now onwards. I applied my voice and faith on a very wrong and bad thing and it happened. Do you also want to bring death with the power of your voice and faith onto your life?

Why can't you just listen to me because I've been there and I'm talking about something that has happened to me? It was proven by the time I went to prison for what I have said and done. Why don't you listen to Jesus's words since you believe in him?

Or you'll only believe all this when it happens to you? I challenge you to think about your past now. You'll see and understand that what I'm telling you is true. You'll see that you have been creating your whole life with your words that you spoke and you believed in them.

Think about it because I'm sure you'll realise what I'm telling you day by day. Jesus concluded by telling them that everything is possible when you believe. We're also told that Jesus asked his disciples on how long must he be with them if they still don't have faith and do the things he could do. This statement clearly shows that Jesus came to earth to show us on how to do things by ourselves, and by the power that we possess inside us.

Isaiah 41:10, God tells you to not have fear because He is always with you and He is **your** God. Now if He is your God, why don't you use Him in the right way to get what you want? Why don't you use Him to claim what's yours and have been waiting for you all this time? God said this because He knows that when fear increases, He decreases. But He is asking you not to have fear at all, because He is **your** God and He will always be with you no matter what.

Isaiah 41:13, He continues telling you that, "**I AM** the Lord, **your** God. **I AM** holding your right hand so please don't be afraid of anything. **I AM** here to help you with **anything** and **everything** that you want." Do you remember who is **I AM**? When you say **I AM**, who are you referring too? Yes, you; it's you who is "**I am**", the real you that is inside your body right now. Do I really need to explain this verse further? Everything is just there, and the only thing you have to do is to open your eyes and see the truth.

Right now in your situation you are in, tell yourself that where you are right now isn't where you'll end up. You do know now that you have all the power inside you and you have been told about the power of your voice; so speak life onto your life and have faith. From now onwards you should direct your life to a direction you want to be in, and by the faith that's within you, everything is possible to achieve.

Tell yourself you have money, even though you don't see it with your physical eyes, but it's there in your spiritual eyes. Open them now so you could see your money that has been waiting so long for you to obtain.

John 6:47, anyone who has faith will live forever. This means that when you have faith you will **live** and be **alive**, but if you don't have faith you are not alive but you are dead. This is life we are living in and you should have faith so you can live; and not only that, you will receive everything that you have ever wished for, and it will all happen through **faith**.

The greatest weakness you have is not believing, but having doubts only. How will the doubts that you have help you? Didn't I tell you if something didn't or doesn't help you must leave it behind you? How can you travel your journey with a baggage that doesn't help you and will also cause you problems in the long run? Have faith in your darkest days and the light will present itself. Whatever you put your faith in, it will be done.

James 2:21-26, Abraham proved his faith by sacrificing his son Isaac on the altar, then God was pleased and he became God's friend. To have faith is not only by saying that you have faith, but you need to prove that you have faith. Having faith that is not put into good use, it's the same like a person who doesn't have faith. Faith needs to be put into **action** and that's when it's called faith. The faith that is not put into action is just as dead. So you need to put faith into action at all times.

No one who has faith will be disappointed with the outcome (1 Peter 2:6). Just like Jesus did, when you have faith, the results are **always** pleasing. The people that

God will accept and work together with, are the people who have faith (Hebrews 10:38). If you don't have faith, nothing can be done.

Faith is the substance of things that you hope for and gives us assurance of what we cannot see (Hebrews 11:1). Through our faith, we know that the earth was made by God's Word, and yet again we know that what can be seen was made by what cannot be seen (Hebrews 11:3). Can you see now that the things that are not seen are so powerful and they make the things we see today?

You were also made by the Spirit. And the Spirit lives in you; something that cannot be seen. When you die the spirit returns to God who gave it. You won't be yourself, but you will be dead in flesh. That means you are really made by something that cannot be seen. You too can create things that can be seen when you use your voice and your faith. The things you want and need is made by what you have right now.

Without faith nothing can be done and your God won't be pleased with you (Hebrews 11:6). That means faith has made everything that you see today. If you belong to God, you should have faith and everything will be made possible (Hebrews 11:30).

Just like the people of Israel had faith in God and so He saved them from Egypt. Faith is not what you feel, but faith is what you do. Believe in yourself and make all things possible with your faith. Don't be faithless, have real faith so God will do things for you (Matthew 6:30).

All that matters in the world is your faith (Galatians 5:6). Abraham had faith in God and God accepted him, and same should apply to you too. If you have faith in God, He will accept you and make everything possible for you.

Let your God lead you through everything and also have faith in Him (Psalms 37:5). Fear will make sure that it paralyzes your spirit, but you need to make sure you have faith to overcome everything. Faith removes fear and doubts because they are not needed in our lives.

Don't let your temporary situation make you lose faith in God. He has already told you that He will never ever leave you and He is here holding your right hand. No one will understand and have faith if they don't believe in the things that Jesus Christ did (Romans 10:17).

I don't walk with what I physically see, but I walk in what I see in faith. Take it from me, all challenges are temporary, just look up and have faith and you'll overcome everything.

Ask God to make you are winner at all times so you'll overcome what you are going through (Psalms 118:25). God is saving all the people who have faith in Him (Romans 1:16). So, don't you want to be saved? If you don't have faith in God, He will test you and He will not wipe out your enemies as He did with the Israelites (Judges 2:20-23).

God only accepts the people who have faith (Romans 3:22). So if you don't have faith, God will never accept you. A person can only be measured with the amount of faith that they have (Romans 12:3). If you don't have faith, you are regarded as a useless person who won't go anywhere in life. When you have faith within you and you also use the faith that you have with the actions that you take, God will accept you (Romans 5:1). Lions may go hungry, but those who have faith in God will never starve (Psalms 34:10). If you really have faith in God; you will never be broke or poor, but you will keep on succeeding, being successful and wealthy all your life.

Let me give you two of my favourite verses in the scriptures. Mark 9:23, **anything** is possible for someone who has faith. Galatians 3:9, **everyone** who has faith will prosper. Just by these two verses, what's more could you ask for or be told?

Anything is possible with someone who has faith, and you will prosper, be successful and be wealthy only if you **believe**. This is the principle and it always works. Just believe in something that you do, and it will be done with very less work put into it.

You need to understand this. Jesus came to this world to bless you. He came to fulfil what God had promised Abraham. And by the faith that you have, you'll receive every blessing from your God. I know that some of you might be asking on how exactly I receive the blessing when I have faith. The answer is so simple, you need to **pray**, have **faith** and take **action**.

When you are thinking about anything, you are praying for what you are thinking about. When you talk about something, you are also praying for what you saying. By the faith that you have, you bring what you have prayed for to you. And then by the action you take, you receive everything that you have prayed for.

Be clear about what you want when you pray, and also be careful of what you think or talk about because you are creating everything you say or think about. Your faith will help you gain possession of the success and wealth that you need in your life (Hebrews 11:33).

2 Kings 7:1-2, Elisha promised that the following day in Samaria they would be enough food for everyone, but the chief officer didn't believe what Elisha was saying. And so the chief officer was promised that he will see it happen but he wouldn't taste the food.

The next day when God blessed Samaria with food, the chief officer saw it happen, but he really didn't even taste the food. He was trampled to death by the crowd who were rushing to collect food from enemy's camp. And just by being faithless, he was killed by the lack of faith (2 Kings 7:18-20).

This story shows that if you don't have any faith, you are good as dead, and you will die. You will see people prosper in front of your own eyes but you won't prosper and you'll eventually die. People didn't believe that Jesus was going to bring Lazarus to life after he had been buried for four days. But Jesus asked them, "Didn't I tell you that when you have **faith**, **everything** is possible to achieve?" (John 11:38-44).

Jesus knew that faith is the foundation of everything, and it's the thing that makes everything possible. He had faith before he even prayed for what he wanted to happen. The faith that Jesus had, plus the prayer that he prayed, brought Lazarus to life, and by the action that was taken when the stone was rolled aside. Jesus received what he prayed for and Lazarus was brought to life.

Again this story tells and shows us the power of a prayer when it's being used with faith and action that is taken. It shows us how is everything possible to achieve when you use the three together. If you do as your God tells you to do, He will make all your prayers possible (Psalms 34:15).

You know, when I look back I could see that I always found a job easily whenever I looked for one. All this happened because I told myself that it was easy for me to get a job, and at that time I was unaware that I was creating what I thought about. And through the faith that I had, I got the job.

If you don't believe in yourself, who else will? I believed in myself and I got what I wanted. You too can believe in yourself so you'll get what you desire.

When the prison warder led Paul and Silas out of prison, he asked them what he needed to do in order to be saved. They replied and told the prison warder to have **faith** (Act 16:30-31). You too can also be raised from the dead if you activate the faith that lies within you right now.

Chapter 10
IMPORTANCE OF A PRAYER

James 1:5-8, if you need something, you better pray to **your** God and He will provide you with what you have prayed for. God is willing to give you more than you have prayed for. He is willing to give you anything freely. He has plenty of what you need. He is unselfish. He is obliging. He is considerate and He will give you abundance of what you have prayed for without any questions. But you must make sure that when you pray for something you don't have any fear or doubt, but have faith only. If you doubt what you have prayed for, you are like a wave driven by the wind in a storm and you'll be tossed around.

You cannot be trusted if you have doubts and therefore you won't receive what you have asked for. You need to make up your mind so you can be trusted and be given what you deserve to receive. If you have doubts, don't expect to receive anything. But if you have faith, expect to receive everything you have prayed for.

Exodus 33:15-16 Moses was asking God for what he wanted Him to do. Then God replied in V.17 and He said, "I will do what you have asked me." This is how the prayer works, ask anything from God and He will answer your prayers with what you have requested from Him.

James 5:15, when you pray for the sick people and you have faith, they will be healed. Faith heals everything around you. Prayer + faith + action= Receiving what you have prayed for now. Delete the belief that God answers in His own time and you should be patient. Remember that God lives in you and you are creating your desires and what you have prayed for.

If you believe that God answers in His own time and you should wait, let me tell you that what you have prayed for will delay because you are creating it to delay by your beliefs. Remember, it took me 9 days to be in the hands of the police, and 10 days to take someone's life after I had asked for it.

You don't necessarily need to kneel and close your eyes when you pray for something. Just by thinking about it or saying it, you will have already prayed for it, and that's what happen to me. I said something unaware that I was praying, asking, requesting or creating for it to happen. And I had to eat every word I spoke.

Now I did a huge mistake by not guarding my thoughts and tongue, and I had to suffer the consequences. But now I'm here to save you from all the trouble that you might go through as well. To be on the safe side of things, just watch and control your thoughts and tongue. These are two things that pray and ask while you are unaware, since you are failing to control them. Just tell yourself that God answers everything now because He really will.

And once you are in control and clear on what you want, don't worry about anything, but pray for everything that you want (Philippians 4:6). Praying will change your life forever and that's for sure. Communicate and talk to your God all the time, He is with you and listening always. He is in you and you can ask Him anything you want, and by faith you shall receive. This is part of praying and requesting to God.

If you don't pray, request and ask God for what you want or need, He won't provide you with those things because you need to profess on what you want and need. You need to request, ask and pray to God for what you want so He will answer your prayers.

2 Samuel 2:1, David had to ask before the Lord could answer what he had asked for. This shows that before you get anything, you need to ask first, than receive. John 11:41-42, Jesus had faith that his prayer will be answered even before he started to pray.

He was also grateful to God that He had already answered his prayer. I have already spoken about gratitude and how it's important to be grateful for everything, and here we see Jesus being grateful and he received what he prayed for in the quickest time through the gratitude he had.

Chapter 11
SERVE GOD TRUTHFULLY

I don't understand why some people think God doesn't want you to be happy and satisfy yourself. God wants you to **enjoy** life and find it **easy** to live. He wants you to have **fun,** be **rich** and accomplish all your **desires.** But most importantly God wants you to **love** and **serve** Him truthfully through His people.

You see, in order to serve other people, you need to serve yourself first, so that you can serve other people with love and joy. Once you have served yourself first and equipped yourself with all the necessary things you need, you can serve other people. Only then can you serve other people with what you have.

You need to acquire whatever skills or position to assist and serve other people. You cannot donate any money in the welfare if you don't have that money yourself. You need to get the money first, before you can even donate the money. You cannot give love if you do not love yourself. You cannot give something that you don't possess, but you can only give something that you have.

Nehemiah 8:10, Nehemiah said to the people, enjoy your food and wine, and then you can share with others. This means you also need to be happy and enjoy what you have, and also share with others. Now here is the trick that some people don't understand. If you want to be really successful and wealthy, you must **serve** other people on this world or your community (Mark 10:43). Be ready to help others at all times (Titus 3:1).

You see, when God makes you successful, He is making you to be like a tap of water. Through the tap the water is always flowing to supply and help people who need water. Bear in mind that the water never stops running because there is a huge tank or dam which keeps supplying you as the tap.

If you stop supplying people with water, you become a useless tap and also the tank as your supplier won't provide you, since you have stopped giving out water as well. This is simple, the **more** you give, the **more** you receive from your supplier who is God. Be like the tap and always be ready to serve the people of God through whatever you have.

Serve God by giving Him your money, crops and anything else that you have. By doing that, you will have more money, crops and everything else that you touch will turn into a success (Proverbs 3:9-10). Now how do you do that because God is a Spirit? You serve Him through His people.

Don't tell someone to come tomorrow for help while you could help him today (Proverbs 3:28). You can become very poor by being greedy, and you can also become successful and wealthy just by giving freely. When you give freely, you will get an incentive for that.

If you give less, you will receive less, but when you give more, you will attract and receive more (Proverbs 11:24-25). God blesses everyone who serves the poor (Proverbs 14:21). When you abuse the poor, you will have God to deal with you. But when you treat the poor with care, God will reward you for that because you have shown respect to Him (Proverbs 14:31).

When you serve or give back 10% of what you earn, you are creating and opening a door of good things to keep flowing in your life. Trust me when I say by doing so, you are really helping yourself. Look at our very own international and late icon DR Nelson Mandela. He was giving away a portion of his salary to help kids and the people of God. And look at how he kept on being successful. Even after he passed away, he left a will and a lot of people benefited from it while they were not even his children. Now that was the best lesson to learn from our icon. Look at how successful Oprah Winfrey is. God made her a tap to supply His people with what they need, and that's why she keeps getting more and more successful herself.

What do you think her secret is to become successful every time and in everything she touches? It's obvious that she's serving God through His people and that's why she keeps getting more herself. I don't know her personally, but from where I stand and watch her on television, she's a woman who is always giving and helping people. Then those people who receive gifts from her would be happy and start to cry tears of joy. Where do you think those tears of joy are going too? They are going towards her success and they will make her more successful. Even if she is using her own money or she's getting sponsors, but the fact is the tears of joy and all the credit goes directly to Oprah.

There is a lot you can learn from her and this too shall help you to be successful in everything you touch. There is no need to give all the 10% of your income to the church you minister in. The point of the 10% is to serve God through His people. You can donate the 10% to welfare, help a neighbour, assist a child in his/her education and clothing, or share the 10% amongst a lot of different people or organizations. The point of the 10% is to help other people and by doing that you are also helping yourself as well by creating a path of giving and receiving. Remember that what you do to others is being done to you.

Let's look at our very own South African businessman and billionaire Patrice Motsepe. He is always giving back millions of Rand not to South Africans only, but to the community of this world. He has joined the world's greatest and richest like Bill Gate and Warren Buffet and many more in giving 50% of his wealth to the needy people of this world when he leaves this world. If you look at the strategy of these people, they always giving out millions and they still getting millions in return on a daily bases.

They have created a path of giving and receiving and that is why they keep accumulating more wealth. All these people understand the power of giving back and serving the people of this world and making a difference. I'm seeing this method of giving back working perfectly and keep making people more wealth, and I don't know about you. If you agree with me, and I'm sure you do, why don't you just adopt this method which will work for you as well? You can learn from these people I have just mentioned and you must walk in their footsteps and just by doing so, you will be allowing more wealth to flow into your life.

Have you ever wondered why the Islam (Muslims) religion is very successful and wealthy? The answer is so simple, the Islam religion still follows the basic laws, and one of them is giving back to the people of God. As I have mentioned above, when you help other people and serve God through His people, you will be basically helping yourself by opening the doors of receiving. The Islam religion is the people who make **sure** that they give back to the community of the world and they don't hold back. They even have an organisation (Gift of the givers) that looks in the matter of giving back to the community we are living in. This is one of the most powerful secret that makes them richer day by day.

Luke 6:38 clearly states that you must give whatever you have to other people and you will receive that same thing in full amount back to you. The same measure you give will be the same measurement you'll receive. Give anything out and you'll obtain the same thing back into your life. Give out more love and you'll receive love directly to your life. Give out money and you'll receive more money into your life. Doesn't the law say you reap what you sow, and like attracts like? God says you reap everything that you sow, and the law of attraction says like attracts like. It's just the same thing. Whatever you put in, you'll definitely get out. Does it look different to you? It doesn't to me, and I tell you for certain, that this law does work, and you will be a wise person when you use it to your advantage. The way you treat other people, will be the same way you will be treated by others. Whatever, and I mean **whatever** you give out, will be the same thing you'll receive upon your life.

Chapter 12
MEDITATE & VISUALISE

Meditate

Thinking and forming a mental picture is more important than the information you possess. Information is what you are familiar and aware of; while thinking views the existing pictures and creating them to happen in your life.

Now, whatever you meditate on should be made a habit, and you should meditate every day for about 5 to 20 minutes.

When you are meditating, you actually communicating with your God and creating whatever you are thinking about to take place.

When you meditate, it should always be done in the present moment. Live in your mind like everything is taking place as it is in that very moment you are in.

Don't force your mind into thinking about something. Just relax and allow things to follow into what you are pursuing.

Don't allow anything to distract you. Be in a peaceful place where you can meditate without any disturbance.

Ok, everyone does it differently and the outcome is just the same. Some people prefer silence when they meditate, and the best time for that is in the early hours of the morning when everyone is sleeping. I personally prefer it with a loud noise of my favourite music, preferably house music pumping in my ears. In this way I get to relax every part of my body while lying on my back with my headsets on my ears and I just jump into the world of imaginary while I create everything I desire.

But you should make sure that you are really relaxed when meditating. You shouldn't think about something else, but you should live in your mind like everything is taking place as it is. You shouldn't be angry because that will be just a waste of time.

Make sure that you don't keep moving during your meditation. Remain still and focus till you are finish.

Whatever you are thinking about will always want to take place and become a reality.

Visualise

Create the emotions for your body and mind to take action.

See yourself doing all the necessary work to get where you want to be.

When you are visualising, you get the time to correct whatever mistakes you did or doing and you're making sure that it doesn't ever happen in your life again.

Create clear and visible pictures in the mind that you want to turn into reality.

The more energy you put into making the pictures into a reality by the way they feel, smell, taste, and look; are the more possibility and opportunity you are creating for them to be turned into a reality and faster.

It is vital to see the people who are involved and every action that a person plays during the time you visualise.

Just like in the movie. You should picture your life as a movie and be part of the movie that is playing. Take part, be an actor, a director, sound engineer and an editor. You must exercise all these characters mentioned above in your movie, whether in the screen or behind the scenes.

Talk to the people around you. Know what you wearing and also know what you are eating.

Talk to the people that you see and are within your visualised world.

See yourself going to an ATM and withdrawing a lump sum from your millions to spend on the people you love. Take note of the feeling as you are holding the money. If you have ever watched the movie which is acted by Bow Wow, "The lottery ticket", you'll see and know how you should feel. See yourself spending the money. If there is a woman you want to impress, or you have been asking her out for the whole year and your answer was only no. Now, having all that money and you charming her with the house you are living in, the cars you are driving and everything else that will make you win her. See her falling for you because of everything that you have. Notice the look in her eyes when she looks at you and how you'll feel after winning a woman that you were longing for your whole life. If it's a celebrity that you love, see yourself spending time with her/him and flashing all the money that you have since you have more than what he/she has. See your perfect wedding taking place with a lot and different other celebrities attending your wedding. See yourself helping in the church you're in when they tell you that they wish to open another branch. You must see yourself helping the poor and being a good example to the rest of the world. Just feel and think about anything that you want to take place because you are creating it to take place.

The emotions that you'll be feeling during the time you're visualising, they will be communicating with your mind and asking it to make everything possible in the quickest time. Notice and understand how it feels to be a multimillionaire, and making all your desires possible. Picture your role model or the most person you admire sitting with you in your house and having a chat with.

See your best musician performing for you and your whole family in your big house. The list is just endless and you know what you need and want. But what I'm saying to you is just to think and create pictures in your mind. Dwell on them during the day and believe that they are really happening in that moment. And when you dwell on them, your mind will follow the command you have set.

Remember, when you are creating something, you don't visualise like it's something that you want to do. You will always want to do that same thing and you'll never get to do it. When you visualise, you must live in that present moment, just like everything is happening now. The mind doesn't know if the things you are visualising on are for real or not. That's why you should be very clear on what you are visualising on, because you are creating for it to take place. The pictures should be very clear just like your home or the car you drive. You know exactly where you live or what type of car you drive. You have seen the engine. You know the colour. You know how your steering wheel feels. You know the smell of your car and you know what type of music you always play and how it makes you feel when driving your car. This is exactly how you should feel and see everything you're visualising on. Although you don't have those things, but see them as if they are yours already; in fact they are yours because you can see them in your mind. The only thing you need to do is to put them on your hand or make them physical for you to use. This is the way to make them a reality it a quickest way. Pictures are more valuable than words. And that's why it's important to keep those pictures flowing in your mind. And make sure that you feel the presence of everything you desire.

You can visualise at any time of the day. I personally visualise everything and all my desires during my bath time, when going to church and when I'm alone. Basically I meditate and visualise whenever I get a chance or not talking to anyone.

Don't meditate and visualise on your past challenges because you are creating space for them to happen to you again. But rather focus on all the promotions that you have ever achieved and by this way you are creating more promotions to occur into your life.

Chapter 13
TAKE ACTION NOW

Think about this, if you had to live for one day and the following day you don't remember anything and you don't own anything from the previous day. You'll have to work for that certain day only and the next day you won't remember anything that you did the day before.

That means if you want to be successful that day, you'll have to wake up early and work or hustle hard for the first few hours of the day so that by the afternoon you will enjoy your benefits of working hard in the early hours of that day.

We would also have the lazy people as well, who would sleep the whole day or half the day and they won't enjoy the benefits of being successful, because all that they do is to sleep or just sit there and wait for hand outs from other people, who have worked hard to earn what they have. So from the two types of people, which one would you like to be?

Now my advice is for you to take action now, not later, but now. Remember that time is only going forward and you can't put it on hold or pause it like a TV game or a

PlayStation. You should keep on moving forward so you will reach your destination in a very short and comfortable time for yourself. Everything is in your hands, do what you have to do today, and tomorrow will be much easier for you. But only after you start from today, NOW!

Moses took action in everything he did with his walking stick and everything he said the Lord God will do was a success. As much as the people healed themselves with faith that they had, Jesus helped those people in the process of healing with the action that he took. Jesus spoke with his voice and laid his hands, and the man was healed (Matthew 8:3).

Being lazy will not help you at all and you will not achieve anything. But when you take action, you will be rewarded for the action that you took and you'll get more than enough in what you worked for (Proverbs 13:4).

You'll hear people say, "This is my year." But only to find out that he/she said the same words last year and the year before that. Let me tell you that it won't be your year until you change what you are doing and put some action. You can't be the same person each year and think something is going to change. You need to change first, so that the year will also change with you.

Faith without action is dead. You can't just sit down where you are and expect God to do everything for you. After you have done the thinking with some emotions put into, you also need to stand up and put some action into it so you can receive what you have asked for.

You need to meet your God half way by putting action into what you have thought about. Just by thinking you have already asked for what you want and God has taken the first step. The second step must be made by you, by the action that you'll take onwards. It's either you go and speak to someone who can help you, or pick up the phone and call people who you think they can help you. Even that phone call is an action taken closer to your dream.

You'll also hear people say, "You need to be a hard worker." Yes this is true, but the hard work is done on the inside of you. Control your mind and think positive things which will help you to achieve your dreams and create your future ahead of you.

Also use your feelings while you are doing the thinking to help you draw your dream closer to you. Now that is where you'll be working hard, inside of you. When you work on the outside by putting action, everything you have worked for in the inside is received.

That is why some people will say they don't work hard, but they work smartly. They had already done the hard work within themselves. Once you have mastered your thoughts and everything that will help you when you think and become your habit, everything will be very easy from there onwards.

Just look at how successful are the people from other countries, who work and live in your country. They know what they want and came to do and they are doing it. They are not lazy like you, but they have taken the necessary actions to better their lives, including their families.

My teachings in this book are based on inspiring you; motivating you; build you up and make you grow. Stretch your strength to your fullest and highest level. Empowering you; opening your spiritual eyes and make you understand how life operates; changes you to become the best and the world's greatest.

What you need to do is to take action and be in control of your life and start thinking success, because no one else will do it for you. You should start talking good and positive things into your own life, since you are the creator of your own life.

Don't have fear when you want to take that action, because fear will make sure that it paralyzes you and it will also make sure that you don't take the action you need to take towards your dreams. Don't even associate yourself with fear, because it brings you down to its own level. And not only that, but it will beat you with experience just like it did to other people.

You need to understand that fear has been in this world for many years and fear has a lot of experience which it is waiting to apply on you. So it's best not to associate yourself with fear at all because you'll go down where it expects you to be. And by that time when fear has finished with you, he will make you his best friend and you'll never be successful.

Let us personify faith as a **she** and fear as a **he**. So now, the choice is yours. Do you take a she or a he? But I'm really hoping from today you'll take the she, because the she is the mother of all nations just like Eve. That means she will give birth to beautiful things in your whole life, and you will be successful and wealthy beyond measure from today onwards. Tell yourself that fear doesn't exist in your life, but she does. Nothing can be done without the she and from now onwards you should be married to her because you really need her in your whole life. Always know that **action + faith = Success**.

The Most High God will never do what you can do for yourself. He has equipped you with the power and He expects you to use the power He gave you from the beginning. 2 Kings 7:3-9, the four men with leprosy knew that if they just sat there and did nothing about their life like you are doing right now, they will die. But they decided to take action, even though they knew that they might win or lose. They knew exactly well that they might die for the action they planning to take, but they also knew that if they just sit and do nothing about their lives, they will die for sure. Then they decided to take the action and save themselves from death. The action that they took saved them from starving to death and they were rewarded by the action that they took. They didn't even fight or put a lot of energy into the action that they took. But they were rewarded at the end. And you too should do the same. You might not need to put too much into your action and succeed. But you'll never know until you try and decide to take action from today.

You can learn a thing or two from an ant. Ants don't have someone to follow them around, but they know that they have to store food during the time of harvest, and they do that. Then I ask you my lazy brother/sister, how long will you have to bear the pain of having nothing in your life and living with hand outs? How long will you sit there and do nothing about your life, while you watch other people succeed? How long can you take that pain you feeling now? At the time I was writing this book, I slept three to four hours maximum, hence I also went to gym for hours. I knew that sleeping is for lazy people who are bankrupt and don't have even a cent in their pocket.

Then again I ask you my brother/sister, how long are you going to just lie there and sleep while you have nothing in your pockets? When are you getting up from that bed of yours and start taking action away from being broke? When you sit, sleep and do nothing, you won't have anything and everything will be gone like somebody had stolen from you. But yet you have stolen your own peace from yourself (Proverbs 6:6-11).

If you lazy, you will be poor and broke. But if you take the necessary action, you will be successful and wealthy (Proverbs 10:4-5). When you are not doing your job properly, you are a liability to the person or company you working for (Proverbs 10:26). Hard working people have more than enough food and money to provide for themselves and family. But daydreamers will be bankrupt and starve to death, because they don't take action like real fools (Proverbs 12:11). If you are lazy, you will always remain a slave to somebody else. They will make you work hard and pay you less money. And you'll continue to work as a slave because you need that small money to survive. But if you apply the things I have taught you in this book and take action, you will be a very successful and wealthy person (Proverbs 12:24).

Yet again, if you are lazy to work for that small amount of money, you will starve to death. A person who continues to work, will have something to eat (Proverbs 12:27). When you talk only with no action, you will still be broke. But if you put action in your plans, everything will be a success (Proverbs 14:23). Every action that you take, you will get an incentive from it, whether good or bad (Proverbs 12:14)

USA is so blessed to have people like Bishop TD Jakes who is so talented and try by all means to take us to the next level. In South Africa we are also blessed to have people like pastor or should I say DR. Sthembiso Zondo. These people speak the Word of God and every time when they do speak, something happens in people's hearts. I listen to the motivations that are on radio sometimes in the morning, and I also listen to a lot of people, people like Pastor Zondo, Jim Rohn, Eric Thomas, Donald Trump, Mel Robbins, Robert Kiyosaki, Joe Vitale, Tony Robbins, Bob Proctor and bishop Jakes and I don't just want everything that they say to just tickle my feelings and do nothing about it. The books that I read and everything that these men said, I applied it, and it took me to where I am today. Most people will hear motivational talks from these people and other powerful people, but those words will just tickle their heart and they will do nothing about the words that were spoken to them. I'm not here to change anything that these men have said, but I'm here to tell you that it's time for you to **take action**. You can't be sitting and dancing to the lovely motivations you hear every day and do nothing about it. Yet you expect miracles to happen in your life.

You have heard what you needed to hear and now it's your time to play your part and use your mind, hands, legs and your voice to take the necessary actions to put you where you need to be. When something positive is spoken to you, you need to take action upon those words, because that's the only way you can achieve all your desires. Listen, and take action. The words that are spoken won't help you at all if **you** don't take action. Don't be like the people who want their hearts to be tickled by words and take no action. Action has the power to change your life forever. If you listen to the words that are written on this book and use them. That is when you will be successful. Some people will sit down and say God will provide for me. Yes, The God that we serve will provide you, **but only** if you take action. And you better take the action **now**!

Chapter 14
STUDY GUIDE

Let's reflect on what I have taught you from the previous chapters, but this time we won't be using the Bible verses. I want us to apply the knowledge I have shared with you daily. Every day you must read three paragraphs and practice them. Meditate and visualise everything based on you. Make sure that you dwell on one paragraph for a few hours before you move on to the next one. I want this chapter to be practical because I need everyone to use the information I just shared with you, because knowledge alone is not helpful at all.

I always hear people say knowledge is power, but I totally disagree with that. Why do I disagree? The answer is simple; because knowledge is not power and it can never be powerful alone; therefore Knowledge is not power, but used knowledge to make a change is so powerful.

PRAYER, FAITH, ACTION

Now before you start with your daily exercise, you need to know that there are only three things which you need to apply in order to make everything a reality They are called **PFA** when they are combined. You need to **pray**, have **faith** and take **action**. And that's when you'll receive what you have prayed for.

When you apply all the other points I have mentioned throughout the book, together with these three factors I'm talking about now. You'll be making everything come to you and be turned into a reality in the quickest speed ever.

Now if you take this root, nothing will hold you back because your life path will be clear and no bad or negative things will be present to stop you from achieving what you desire. You will feel free, lighter and you'll attract everything that you desire into your life.

Now let's begin…

IF YOU WANT TO ALTER YOUR CURRENT LIFESTYLE, START BY ALTERING THE WAY YOU THINK: The only thing that's holding you back from now to achieve your goals, it's the way you think now and how you were thinking before. Since your thinking has never helped you or has placed you in the situation you are in right now; just change the way you think from now onwards. Think in a different and an opposite way from the way you were thinking yesterday.

TRULY BE GRATEFUL TO GOD FOR ALL THE THINGS THAT YOU CAN SEE IN YOUR MIND: This is the way that will show that you truly have faith. When you apply your faith to the things that you can see in your mind, every single one of them will be turned into a reality, and will come to existence into this world where your physical eyes can see. Whatever you own in your spiritual eyes, can be owned in your physical eyes.

TURN EVERY ACTION INTO A SUCCESS: Understand that every power comes from within and you should make it work for you. Everything that you touch, speak or think about; make it work for you and turn it into a success.

EVERY ACTION YOU TAKE IS EITHER GOOD OR BAD: Know that there is no action which won't get any reward. Every small or big action that you take will be rewarded. When it is a good action, you will be rewarded for it, and you will be successful and wealthy.

FEEL LOVED AND ADMIRED: Everything is done with love. You need to love and admire yourself. And then know that everybody loves and admires you; and I mean everybody, including the people you say they are your enemies. Know that the word enemy does not exist at all. Don't say or think that you have enemies, just know that everybody loves and admires you.

FOCUS ON THE CHANGE AS YOU ARE BECOMING MORE AND MORE SUCCESSFUL: Take note of everything that is happening in your life and be grateful when you see a small change taking place. That small change is the start of big things to come. Focus on what you are becoming day by day and congratulate yourself. You'll need to focus and concentrate on everything as you are reaching for your success on a daily bases.

THE TONGUE HAS THE POWER OF LIFE & DEATH: I have explained to you on how I wrote my future with my tongue, and it is important for you not to do the same mistakes I did, since I'm giving you this study guide of life. Know that every time you think, write or talk, you are holding a pen which is writing your future, and everything that is written down **will** take place. Make a decision now that your tongue will be a pen of a skilful writer who writes with wisdom from the mind.

THE WAY YOU SHOULD THINK FROM NOW ONWARDS: You must conceive and form a mental picture. Shape the appearance of the picture you are visualising on. Edit it and make it the shape, colour and everything else that you wish it to be. Develop the picture and organize it to be something that you want it to be, and live inside the picture you have created for yourself, because it will take place sooner than you think. Just make everything for yourself with a divine mind.

THINK IT, HAVE FAITH AND RECEIVE IT: When you think about something, you are creating it to take place. By faith that you have, you are bringing it to yourself and by the action that you take, you will receive it.

DO IT WITH A VISION: Every action you take should be done with the vision in mind. As you are putting action, hold your vision in your mind and make sure it's always with you. The action and the vision should be your best friends and be applied together at all time.

BLOCK ALL THE DISTRACTIONS: It is very important to block everything that could distract you whenever you are pursuing something. It's also important to block all distraction when you meditate and visualise. When you are thinking, praying, asking, requesting and creating what you desire, it is important to focus in that current state and don't allow any other thought to come crawling into your mind. You might have seen the sign "Please do not disturb" in hotel rooms, and that is a sign you should wear when you are creating your reality. All the other unwanted thoughts should see this sign and turn away. You shouldn't allow or dwell on unwanted thoughts when you pray. Ask and create your future with pure thoughts that will assist you in getting your request. Just like in your computer, two of the same program cannot run at once. You need to run one program till it's finished so it can maximise its performance. Your computer can never run two anti-virus programs at the same time and maximise or expect your computer to be super clean or function properly. They just can never work properly when you want to use them both. You need to uninstall one, so you can use the one you have chosen. Same thing applies with your mind. When you want to achieve your desires to your maximum abilities, you need to uninstall all the unwanted thoughts and run a mental program that will create only pure thoughts for yourself.

DO NOT WORRY ABOUT THE PAST, BUT FOCUS ON THE FUTURE: You are not the only one who has a past. We all do, but you must know and understand that yesterday is gone and will never return. Today is here and the future is coming. Don't beat yourself up and don't worry yourself about yesterday's mistakes because you can never fix them. You rather put your focus on today and the future because that can rectify the mistakes you did yesterday. Don't worry about it whether they were right or wrong yesterday, but focus on doing it right today.

DON'T WORRY, BE HAPPY: Make sure you don't worry about anything and just focus on being happy at all times. You don't need to know how everything will happen or take place, just focus on being happy and know that God has got you covered.

THE KEY TO EVERYTHING: Know that everything that you do today and onwards is the key to your successful and a wealthy life.

BECOME A SUCCESS TO BE SUCCESSFUL: Become grate now, so you'll be the greatest tomorrow. You will never get what you want and you'll be looking for it till forever, if only you don't change and be what you want. As I have said, everything starts from the inside and so you should be what you want to be. Be a success, so you'll be successful. Think of success, so you'll be successful. Just know that you become who you are (you are what you are). When you see yourself as being broke, you will always be broke. But when you see yourself rich, you will be rich. Therefore you will become what you want to be in future. All the things you want are made by **YOU**.

THE REAL YOU: 99% of who you are, the inner man; he cannot be seen or touched and he is invisible. The scripture has told you that your body is a tent and all the power comes from within and therefore under your

221

control. Success and wealth comes from within, simple as that.

MONEY IS YOUR BEST FRIEND: Remember that you have limited things to do without money. If you will render good service to people, you'll need money. When you want to travel around the world, you'll need money. When you think about food, you'll need money. You must know that everything that you do rotate in circles around the money, and the money rotates in circles around everything that you do.

YOU ARE THE BANK AND THE MONEY IS THE REAL YOU: Know that you are the origin of money; you are the true supplier of all the money, and you are the bank which keeps lots of millions in it. Your mind is the bank and all the money stays in your bank, and it's now up to you to use the money that you have.

EVERYWHERE YOU GO, TELL YOURSELF: Some people are just negative about themselves and they have a low self-esteem, but it's time to change that now. Speak to yourself and put commands that you'll know and follow. Say something like, I am unique; I am attractive; I have a faithful partner; I have the power to change everything; I always make the right decision; I am god and the creator of everything. Then you must truly mean, believe and feel what you are saying is true about yourself. And that's when you'll see a change and those things you have said about yourself will really come true and a reality to yourself. Feeling happy and believing what you are saying to yourself will make provision for it to take place sooner than you think.

DO THE RIGHT THING AND DON'T WORRY ABOUT ANYTHING ELSE: Just do everything as instructed and don't worry about how is the thing that you prayed for is going to come to you. Don't worry about when will it come to you, and don't worry about if everything will be possible to obtain no matter if it's too big. The three things I have just mentioned take care of themselves when you apply everything accordingly. To achieve these things in the quickest time, it will be shown by the energy you have invested in what you want.

WHEREVER YOU INVEST YOUR POWER AND ATTENTION ON; IS EXACTLY WHAT YOU'RE GOING TO GET BACK: Place it on cars, you'll get more cars. Place it on money, you'll get more money. Place it on helping others; you'll get more help from other people yourself. Place it on being happy, you'll get more happiness in your life. Again, you will reap what you have sown and the like attracts like.

YOU WILL BECOME WHATEVER YOU THINK YOU ARE: Have you noticed that if you think you are a failure, you really become a failure? But when you know that you'll make it through, you are going to make it through? Whatever you tell the mind to do, the mind will do. The mind doesn't know anything, it just gets the commands from you and the mind will apply your commands every time.

TIME FOR A CHANGE: Now this is a very exciting part. It's very simple, trust me it works perfectly. Just like everything that is stated in this book. If you really want to change something in your life that you don't like; go into the world of imagination and change that thing to something that you want it to be. Isn't that wonderful news that we can now edit our lives more especially when we can see that in the long run we will equip ourselves with difficult challenges? Yes, this is just amazing; the only reason you couldn't do it before it's because you were not aware of it. But now you do. If you just give yourself time and feel what you are doing, you will change your life forever. Try it; you have nothing to lose after all.

YOUR TRUE PARTNER: Know that you are in a relationship with money, and money is your partner. Share the love that you have with your partner every time and make sure the connection is there. Communication is the key to any kind of relationship, and therefore you should communicate with the money that you have right now. Build your relationship that you have with the money and also grow in loving it. In this way the money will build its relationship with you, and it will make sure that it grows in love with you. And what does that mean for you? Happy! That means more money is coming your way, only because you have built a solid foundation for your relationship with the money. Say something like, "I love you money my sweet heart", and definitely sure the money will also reply in its own language; a language that you will understand once you have built a relationship with your partner, your money. Hence, the Bible says you can't worship two masters, and that's not the case here. What you are really doing here is showing abundance of love like you'd do with any kind of relationship. That is what God wants after all, to show love and appreciation to everything around us. Love brings happiness and it is the true source to everything. Love your money so you'll get the love from it in return; which means more money for you.

BE GRATEFUL TO THE MONEY YOU HAVE: Make sure that you are grateful for the money that you have, and keep receiving. You must know that you are receiving money every day and every minute of the day. Show appreciation to the money, thank it for coming to you and be grateful for the presence of it. In this way you'd be attracting more money to come to you, but not for a visit, but to stay with you permanently.

BE GRATEFUL TO GOD: Thank God for everything that you have. Thank Him for the blessings that you receive, and also thank Him for the blessings that you will still receive. Just be grateful for everything around you.

EVERYWHERE YOU GO, TELL YOURSELF: There are no limitations and nothing can stop me to be what I want to be. I have unlimited powers to do everything I desire. I can do everything with the power of my mind, and everything is possible to achieve.

I LOVE MYSELF: Everything starts from within you. If you don't love yourself, who else will? Or do you expect people to love you while you don't even care about yourself? If you don't love yourself, how will you even know that you have love within you? What it is that you love more than yourself? Now this is a topic which you should really think about. All these years I also thought that I loved myself, but I was lying to myself because I didn't. If I really loved myself I couldn't have done all the terrible things I did to myself. I did a lot of horrible things which no one could have done if they truly love themselves, and even worse because I never saw anything wrong while I was doing those things. Now if you really love yourself, you need to sit down and check if you really love yourself. Check if you are doing something that you are not proud off. It could be you are doing it because you need money or because you are trying to please someone while you are losing yourself in the process. Just remember that everything is done and brought to life with the love that you withhold within you, and if you don't love yourself, you have lost the basics.

EVERYWHERE YOU GO, TELL YOURSELF: I have money; I have successful businesses; I dress well; I am funny, and just tell yourself about everything you want to be. Record it in your mind and press repeat whenever you get time, and you'll be amazed from the results.

I AM: I have explained the power of I am and who is I am. From now onwards be careful when you use the words I am, and more especially what is going to follow after you say I am. So from now onwards, whatever you want to achieve or be, put I am at the beginning of your sentence. I am rich; I am successful; I am wealthy; I am love; I am helpful; I am happy. So whenever you say whatever you'll be saying, you must mean and believe it. See yourself as already being what you are saying. With the power of I am, you are driving whatever you have said to come to you in the fastest speed.

WHEN YOU THINK YOU CAN DO IT, YOU WILL DO IT ONLY WHEN YOU BELIEVE: Just by thinking that you can do it, that means you really can and you will achieve it when you believe in yourself. It makes it even easier when there are quite a few people who have also done it. They started everything just like you, in the mind; and they did it because they believed in themselves. You can do it too, and you are just at the starting point. So don't wait, go for it. I'm sure you wouldn't want to live with regrets which will hunt you all your life, which will keep saying; what if I did it? I would be living the life of the rich and helping people. Why didn't I even try? Look at that person, he did it and that was my dream. Let me tell you that you better aim for the moon, than not to aim at nothing at all. You have nothing to lose, just try it. And maybe next month it will be you on the front cover on the Forbes magazine.

DON'T WAIT FOR TOMORROW. BUT DO IT TODAY BECAUSE TOMORROW STARTS TODAY: This is a very important point to apply when you want to be successful. Some people will wait for tomorrow to take actions while they have a chance today to do so. You will find people postponing what they can do today, to tomorrow, next week or next month, till eventually they do nothing about it. These people keep postponing because they don't understand that tomorrow will always start today. You cannot just be something better today, if you didn't start yesterday. Your tomorrow will definitely start today. You can never start tomorrow and achieve what you desire that same day, only because tomorrow starts today. And that is when you will achieve all your desires tomorrow since you had made your start today. When you think about it now, do it now.

THINKING CONTROLS EVERYTHING: The reason that you can even think about it, should tell you that you can do it. Everything was created with the mind, and everything that you see today and in front of you now, was created by the mind; the equipment and tool you have right now with you. The only difference between your mind and the mind that created everything that you see right now, is that the people who created the things you can use today, understood that the mind doesn't sleep and they had to keep thinking till they could find something that they can invent. It's your mind, which is just **too** lazy to think. The only bridge between success and failure is the thinking substance. You must know that the mind is the communication of everything that you can see and touch, and therefore you too should start your communication with everything around you. Don't wait for tomorrow, start now and make everything happen for you.

LOVE BRINGS EVERYTHING CLOSER TO YOU: Love is the motivation of everything you want to achieve or be. Everything that you want to be or have should be motivated by the love you have for it. Nothing can be done without love. Make sure you create a path for love in everything that you do. Learn to love everything and everyone, because the source of everything is the love that you withhold within yourself. If there is no love, nothing can be achieved, but if there is love, everything can be achieved.

HAVE FAITH: Having a strong belief is what makes everything possible to achieve. When you think about something and you know that you will do or achieve it, it will be done. When you have confidence and you know that it's possible to achieve, it will be achieved and there is no way it can't be achieved. Think it, believe it, take action and receive it.

CONTROL YOUR MIND: The mind is something that creates habits. Anything that you focus on every day will become your habit and will be turned into your reality. When you are visualising on something, make sure that you search and explore every corner of it and don't leave any details out of the picture. Examine everything thoroughly and don't allow your mind to wriggle out of the picture you are forming. Complete everything in your mind, be happy with what you have created and turn it into the world of your physical eyes.

IT IS VITAL TO ALLOW YOURSELF TO BE SUCCESSFUL: You need not to withhold yourself back by anything that you talk, think or do. From now onwards you should set yourself free and be a free person from all the obstacles that were holding you back in achieving your goals. Feel free and feel happy at all times, and you'll be amazed of the results you'll get.

TAKE GOOD CARE OF YOUR IDEAS: Every idea needs time and attention to grow vigorously. It must be grown and developed very well in order for it to prosper. Just like every plant that you have planted. You need to take very good care of it, so it can be the plant that you expect it to be. If you don't take good care of the plant, it will eventually wither and you would have wasted your precious time. Same thing applies with an idea. You need to take good care of it, so it will grow to what you expect it to be. You need to water and feed the idea with the best nutrition so it will become a very strong and powerful idea that has ever been.

EVERY WORK YOU DO WILL GET A SALARY AT THE END: The effort you put in, is the same effort you'll get out. Whatever you work for, you'll get a salary for it at the end of the month. Just like you have a contract with your employer, and you get a certain salary at the end of the month for your services that you have rendered. Same thing applies with your mind. It says that, "I'm your employer and I will pay you a salary for every service that you render to me." The mind is your boss and your boss is very rich and wealthy beyond measure. He is willing to give you all the money that he possesses for whatever services you will submit to him. The contract that you have with your mind, is not based on a fixed salary, but it's upon the service and effort you present to your boss. If you work for a short time with less work done, you'd be paid less. But if you work for more hours with a lot of work done, you will be paid more. The harder you work the more money you'll get. When you are loyal and dedicate your all to your boss, he will pay you with everything that he has. And you can't know how much he possesses until you keep giving all your best. He will keep paying you for what you submit to him. Your boss knows everything and you can't cheat on him. Whether good or bad, every work has remuneration at the end, and it's only a matter of time before you get paid for all that you have done. Some people are already dead, due to the services that they rendered. Some are in prison for their services as well, and some are in hospitals for their work that they have been doing all these years. But you are blessed enough that you are still alive and healthy; and have not yet been paid for your services. You better alter now before it's too late, because your pay cheque is also coming your way. Rather convert your pay cheque now, so that when it gets to you, you will be the happiest person on earth. Please don't be ignorant just like I was, the choice is yours now.

EVERY DAY COMES WITH NEW OPPORTUNITIES: There are millions of opportunities that are still needed to be discovered, and your mind is here to discover them. You only need to discover one opportunity that can presents itself to you, and you could be a multibillionaire from today. You have all the equipment to be a billionaire and the choice is left with you now. Do you choose to be a multibillionaire or you choice to be broke forever? Think about all the pain you have now all because you don't have money. Do you want this pain to last forever? If you choose not to take steps now and you want to be broke and poor forever, I am giving you a name that will match your character. That name is (Brokey). But if you want to be called (Richey Rich), that is the best decision you have made. Just don't be like Brokey, and go out there and live your life to the fullest. Brokey will always be there to praise and talk about you day and night. Brokey will be living your life with just the talks, but no action. Remember that your mind is with you to help you create anything so you can become wealthy. Again, there are millions of opportunities that have never been created before, and you can make a change by inventing at least one. By doing so, you will be able to fly and help everyone you have always dreamed to help.

MEET YOUR BLESSINGS HALFWAY: You can't just sit there and expect that God will just bless you with everything since you believe in Him. You need to get up and meet Him halfway with the actions you'll take in order to be rewarded. To be blessed is when the promotion meets your preparedness. You have to be prepared in order for you to meet your blessing. Position yourself in the right place from now onwards so you'll be blessed tomorrow.

SERVE YOURSELF FIRST: Before you can serve someone else, you must service yourself first. How can you upgrade someone while you need to be upgraded yourself? Everything starts with you, and rubs off to the next person. You just cannot buy someone a house while you need a shelter yourself. You need to get yourself a proper home, than you can buy someone a house. Upgrade yourself first before you can upgrade somebody else. The most important service you can render to somebody is to service yourself first.

BE WHAT YOU WANT TO BE: People always want to be something better in life, but they don't change what they have been doing for years. You just cannot be something else, while you are still the same person who is doing the same things over and over again. If you want to be something better, you need to change and be someone better. Just be the best that you can be.

YOUR WORD VS. YOUR MIND: When you learn to control every input, you will control your output as well. Everything that you see or hear is being recorded in your mind, and everything you speak is the product of what you are, and the outcome of what you have been loading the mind over the past years. When you choose the people you hang around with, you would have taken the first step in changing your whole life. The people you sit and talk with on a daily bases, have a strong impact of who you will become tomorrow. Your thoughts control the income of everything, and your tongue control the outcome of everything.

HOW CAN I BE SUCCESSFUL: I have explained above that knowledge alone would never help you to become that person you want to be. But applied knowledge will make you a success. Now, to be successful, you need to obtain the knowledge I have given you, use and apply it into positive action, and that is when you will become successful and wealthy beyond measure.

Success is you: Don't look outside, because all the equipment and success is within you. Success is you and therefore within you. Your future that you have dreamt of and still looking for is within you right now. You are holding and traveling with your future everywhere you go, and all this time you never knew that till today. Lucky for those who did knew. What have you done about that all this time? You don't need to pay anybody for them to make you successful or help you to be wealthy. You already are successful and wealthy if you believe so, and you just need to take action. You need to realise that your future is alive inside of you right now. And you just need to put it on the outside world so you can use and enjoy your future you hold inside of you.

HAPPINESS IS EVERYTHING: When you are always happy, you make every good thing come looking for you. When you have created the path of happiness and laughter, all your desires will flow easily into your life. When you are always happy, you are stimulating and putting energy to your success.

THE POWER TO DO THINGS: The power that lies within you is greater than everything that you can see. All was created by this power and the power is greater than everything else. The power is the Spirit, and truly God who creates everything that you can see and touch. The world was created by this power, and therefore the power will always remain powerful more than everything, and most importantly the power is within you and it's truly you. All your life you didn't take note that the secret to do everything is within you. Now it's the time to give it a test and try to see if what I'm telling you will really work. The power is you, so just live your life like you should and you'll be amazed of the outcome.

EVERYWHERE YOU GO, TELL YOURSELF: I am smart; I am fun to be with; people love me; I love myself; I enjoy life; I appreciate life; I am a loving partner; I am the best parent. When you tell yourself all these things and believe it, they will become a reality and your life will be much easier than before. Make sure that you're also thankful for every word you speak to life since everything you speak takes place.

MAKE YOURSELF PURE: Cultivate yourself because your mind is always waiting for whatever instructions you give it. You need to make yourself a pure person who creates only pure things in your life. Cultivate yourself and be a Holy person who has created a path of every good thing to flow into your life. Do not have obstacles which will hold you back in getting what you should obtain tomorrow.

EVERYWHERE YOU GO, TELL YOURSELF: I am good in having conversations with people; I am very creative; I am the best in everything that I do; I want more than enough money so I can get everything that I want and change people's lives; I want my business to prosper; I am born to be rich.

THE MIND WILL ALWAYS TAKE YOUR COMMANDS: Your mind is like a fertile soil and it accepts any kind of seed you will plant in it. You just cannot plant an apple seed and receive an orange tree. You will receive an apple tree just like the seed you sowed. And when you sow an orange seed, you will also receive an orange tree. You will always reap what you have sown. Don't be surprised when you're in challenges because you have created them to take place. And when you have become successful, you should be happy because you made everything possible for yourself. You are the commander and chief of your mind.

EVERYWHERE YOU GO, TELL YOURSELF: I am generous; I support my family and friends in every way; I am born a multimillionaire; I am living my dream; there is success everywhere around me; my success and wealth helps a lot of people; I am a safe driver; I understand myself.

NOTHING JUST HAPPENS: You must take note in everything that is happening in your life because there is a purpose for that thing which is happening to you. Every action that happens in your life is a step closer to your goals. Take note and be grateful for everything that happens whether good or bad because you are meant to go through that situation before you reach your destination.

LIVE IT: You must know that you attract good things into my life; feel confident; praise the people who needs to be praised; recognise every success in your life; find things to be happy for.

WE ARE ALL THE RESULTS OF OUR DECISIONS WE MADE: Nothing just happens. You first came to a situation which needed you to decide, and that decision you took brought change, and today you are living the life your decision has taken you too. Now, in order for you to change your life tomorrow, it will all depend on the decision that you take from now onwards.

EVERYTHING IS EASY: It's so easy to be a businessman; you only need to **think** that you are already a successful business person and you will be a successful and wealthy business person. If you want the biggest house, just **think** of living in that house you want. And in order to have and achieve anything that you desire in life, just **think** and you will live it.

EVERYTHING IS EASY: It's so easy to be a businessman; you only need to **feel** that you already a successful business person and you will be a successful and wealthy business person. If you want the biggest house, just **feel** yourself living in that house you want. And in order to have and achieve anything that you desire in life, just **feel** the presence of that thing and you will live it.

BE CAREFUL: Everything that you're thinking about right now is creating your future. If it's something that has happened before, you are recreating it to take place and happen again. That's why you'll find bad or good things keep happening over and over again to certain people. It's because of the way they think and believe. Think about the good and it will keep taking place in your life and you will be glad that you did.

YOU ARE THE DRIVER OF YOUR OWN LIFE: Your past can never control your future, but only your mind can. If you don't like something, change the way you think and it will also change. The mind is the only thing that can drive your future. Be a skilful driver and use this book to drive and control your whole life.

DO YOUR RESEARCH: While in prison, I'm staying in a place called a special care unit. This place is made for high profile people, people who were policemen, politicians, lawyers, doctors and so forth. Basically it's a place for protection. In this place I had my own room and I stayed alone. This is where I got a lot of time to observe, think and edit my life. I came to a point where I saw that I had created everything that had ever happened to me and all these things kept recurring in my life. I started to change my thinking, actions and basically all habits. In a very short time I started to see a huge change in my life. This time I was doing things differently and my whole life had changed for the better. I came to realise that to change my current situation, I only needed to change the way I was thinking. Now I also challenge you to look back into your own life and you'll notice how the same experiences keep occurring onto your life. Everything is happening the way it's happening because of your thoughts and beliefs. Find time and really think about everything in your past and you'll see that you were the one who created every single thing in your life. I only got the time to think while I am in prison, but you are blessed to have someone like me to inform you about this information while you still have a chance. Come on, find a perfect time for you to think. Don't think for only one day, but think for few days since more thoughts will come pouring into your mind. I normally do the thinking at night or the early hours of the morning while everyone is sleeping. I also play music because it helps me to think deeply. But you can do it anyhow, the point is just to think and I promise you that you will be shocked when you find out that you were busy creating your future with an unconscious mind, and everything kept on recurring onto your future. You have nothing to lose, just think and you'll discover a lot of things about yourself. When you create a perfect time for yourself, you will even heal yourself just by thinking. You might find other things that are painful as you think, but the pain you'll feel should be released afterwards. Some things will make you smile and even ask yourself why you didn't know about all this before. But you only created your life to read this book now, and now it's the perfect time for yourself to start the change. So go on and think...

THE MIND AS THE FOUNDATION: The mind should develop the beliefs and the beliefs should develop some actions. This is the process that should be followed in getting what you desire.

MAKE A HABIT OF WRITING: Write short sentences that you will remember easily on your daily bases and those sentences should be written in the present tense. Write a sentence like "I am rich" or "I have money." I have already explained to you how powerful is I AM, who is I AM and how super powerful are the words that will follow I AM. Learn to talk to the inner man and make him your best friend that you talk to every day and every hour.

START GOING TO BEAUTIFUL PLACES: Just like having friends that are successful and rich, their wealth rubs off on you as well. Now when you visit relatives or friends, make it a habit that you normally visit the ones with beautiful houses and cars. While you are at their place, think about as everything is yours and you own it. Feel the joy of having everything your friend owns and feel the joy of using it. Live in the moment and imagine like everything you see and touch is yours already. This is another method that will make your dream house; cars and everything else come to you in the quickest time ever. I tell you for certain that all that you have imagined and felt, will eventually rub off into your life as well.

APPRECIATE EVERYTHING: Make it your habit that everywhere you go you appreciate things around you. When you see a person driving a beautiful car don't be jealous and say negative things about that car or person, because you'll be chasing away cars that might be coming to you at a later stage. But rather appreciate the car and the person who is driving the car. Appreciate other people's success and speak with them about their success if it's possible for you to do so. Just by appreciating all these things, you are attracting things into your life that you will appreciate and be grateful for. Keep appreciating and you'll be amazed of the outcome.

THE HOW IS NOT UP TO YOU: Just like I created my future to be in prison, I never knew how it was going to happen and I thought it was never going to take place. But the fact that I had already created my future to be in prison by what I said, the **how** took care of itself. What I had already sowed, I had to reap. The same principle always works with everyone. The minute you create your future by your thoughts and beliefs, the **how** will present itself in a way you thought it could never happen; but yet it happens. The **how** works in a very unique way which no person could understand, but only what you have created for yourself can understand the **how** because they work together and can never be separated. The creation works now, and the **how** will come visit you tomorrow. The **how** will come with the action that you'll take and your reality will be present and you will live in it as you created it.

HOW I ATTRACTED MY JOB I USE TO DO: One of my friends was working for one of the cell phones service provider. He asked me if I wanted the job and he told me that I will earn R3000 per month. I wasn't working at that time, but I knew that I can't waste my time in a job that will pay me so little. I knew that I was worth more than that and I could only work if my start salary will be R5000 per month. So I didn't take the job offer, but always visits him whenever he was at work. Sometimes I stayed the whole day at his work place, till I knew everyone including his boss. I wanted to work at the head office of this company because I knew that they earned more than R3000 I was offered. I knew that at the head office I will be paid more than the double amount and I just had to push to get there. One day I spoke to my friend's boss about working at the head office and he told me to email my CV to him, hence this is not the routine to take when you want to work at the head office. One day I got a call and I was told to come for an interview. I knew that just by that phone call, I had already got the job. I knew that when I'm given a chance for an interview, I will make it through no matter what. I did tests, interviews and training and I made it through everything just as I told my mind that I was going to work for this company. I was now working for the company I wanted to work for and I was getting paid more than enough money, and I was just happy. I was clear from the start what I wanted to do and I got the job. Now, I'm telling you my story because I want you to be in control of your life as well. Whatever you do, you need to be clear and aim up high. It doesn't mean that if everyone fails you will also fail. You are different and no one is like you. A new history can be created by you if only you take the step forward from today. Tell your mind what you want and inform it that you are going to do it and get there. I tell you for certain that whatever you told your mind, will eventually take its place. It doesn't have to be the normal root that everyone takes, but if you really know what you want and where you need to be, you will get there dark or blue.

MIND VS. LEGS: Your legs work similar to your brain. When you are sitting down and you are not walking, your legs are useless because you are not using them. And when you get up to fight someone, your legs help you to cause trouble. But when you get up and go to the kitchen to drink some water, that's when your legs became helpful and useful. Same principle applies with your mind as well. When you are just daydream about stupid things all day, your mind becomes useless because it's not helping you at all. But when you start thinking about positive things and creating your success, that's when your mind becomes helpful and useful. You need to use your mind to create success for you, not to create trouble for yourself. Make your mind work for you at all time.

YOU HAVE IT: You have been told in the scriptures that Jesus is your brother and he had the power to change the world and still till today the world is talking about him. You too have that same power that Jesus had right inside you as I speak. He also said it himself that if you have faith, you can do everything that he did and you can do even greater things. You have the strength within you right now to change the whole world. You too are also competent to transform yourself and everything around you. Make the person who is inside work for you so that the future generations will also talk about you thousands of years later.

TURN YOUR KNOWLEDGE INTO A SALARY: Like I said above, knowledge is not power and it can never be powerful alone. Therefore knowledge needs some actions to make it powerful. You won't get any reward for your knowledge unless you do something with it that will reward you at the end. It's pointless to have something and don't use it at all. So it's better to use what you have and obtain something that will work for you tomorrow. In short, use what you have to get what you want and make your knowledge work for you.

EVERYTHING WORKS TOGETHER: Every challenge I went through during my journey has brought me to where I am today. If I didn't go through all those challenges, this book was not going to be possible. I am grateful for every challenge I went through because it has bought me to where I am today. You too shouldn't think that it's over with you. Let me tell you that where you are right now it's the beginning of your real life. God works in situations when everybody has forsaken you and that is where He starts His job. Your life journey was created by you and you are the only person who will create your way out from the situation you in right now. And you are also the only one who will create success for yourself, no one else will, but yourself.

YOU NEED TO MAKE A CHANGE: A car has a steering wheel to be controlled in the direction that you want the car to go. The plane and the ship also have something that controls their destination in order to get there safely. Through all the bad choices you made just like I did, there is always a turning point you should take by the next **decision** you will make from now on. You need to activate the presence of God into your life and let Him direct your life journey. Remember that the spirit you have, is the one that is creating every experience you are going through. I'm here to ask you to please activate the Holy Spirit within you.

KEEP MOVING FORWARD: You can never change your past and there is no need to sit and dwell on something that you cannot change. We are the products of our past, but we can only control the present and future. That's what you need to focus on, the present and future. A car always keeps moving forward, and when it breaks down, you fix it so it will keep moving. Life is like that as well. When challenges come to visit you, you need to fix them and keep moving. That's why the rear-view mirror is small and the windscreen is bigger. It's an example how you should live life, not to dwell on the past, but focus on the future and what's ahead of you.

BE LIKE A CHILD: Whenever you used to fall down as a child, you got up and tried walking again. No matter how many times you fell, you still got up and you didn't even care if someone was laughing at you after each time you fell, but you got up every time till you got it right. So, even when you have become an adult, no matter how many times you fall, you must always have the courage to stand up and face your challenges and keep trying till you get it right. With this book I have given you a guide and manual on how to walk without failure. Again, a child acts and behaves like someone who is perfect at all times. A child has pride and believes in doing something till it gets it right. A child is not afraid to ask for what he/she wants. A child will always express the feelings. You would know if the child is happy, sad or angry. Even the person sitting next to you in a taxi would recognise your child's feelings at that moment with the actions of the child. A child forgives easily and doesn't hold grudges. If you hit a child now, in less than one hour the child would come back to you and a child would want you to play with him/her. A child doesn't look back in the past, but only focuses on the present and future that is ahead. A child would ask you to do a party for him/her, even if a child keeps on asking you to do a party for years and years, but he/she will never give up till you make that party. A child knows what's right and wrong, and you'll find him/her looking at you before he/she does something wrong; just to check if you are watching or not. A child is never afraid of looking ahead and facing the future. The list is endless and there are a lot of things you can learn from a child. I challenge you to watch the actions and notice the words a child speaks. You'll be amazed of the things you can learn from a child. It's time for you to face life like a child and not being afraid of everything. Just be like a child and be happy at all times so good things will start flowing into your life.

TALK TO THE INNER MAN: It is important to communicate with the inner man who is right inside you. He can hear you and understands everything. You need to work with him, and not against him. You need to apologies every time you have done something wrong. Say **"I am sorry"** and apologies to yourself for doing things wrong. Maybe you were angry and said evil words to somebody, you need to come back and apologies to yourself and that person. Just by saying evil words, you have created them to come and visit you. Therefore, that's why it's important to apologies after you have recognised your mistake. You just can never move forward if you don't start to apologies to yourself and forgiving yourself. Forgiving is the key to everything in your life. You need to forgive and release the pain that you have within, so you can bring new and fresh things into your life. If you want to buy a new bed for your house or home, you need to get rid of the old bed and create a space for the new bed to come in. Same applies to you. You need to release all the pain so you can allow all the success you need to flow into your life. Forgive, release and receive.

TALK TO THE INNER MAN: It is also important to acknowledge everything that the inner man has done for you. You need to say, "**Thank you** for everything that you have done for me". Showing appreciation and gratitude will draw more things into your life that you will be grateful for and appreciate. Just like when a person says, "thank you". From the bottom of the heart, you feel so good after that person says thank you and you just want to help them the next time. Same with God, He wants to bless you with more things that you will be grateful for when you say thank you to Him. Open your mouth and just be grateful for everything around you and start thanking people as well. When you are grateful, you'll always be connected with the inner man.

TALK TO THE INNER MAN: Now as I told you that love is the centre of everything, and it brings everything to you when you obtain the love of that thing. You need to assure yourself. Tell God at all times that you love Him, tell Him that you love Him through everything. Say "**I love you** and I will always will". When you really mean and feel that you love God and He notices that, He will want to do everything for you. Just by informing and sharing the love with your God, He will start doing things for you. Remember that all the power comes from within; from God, whether you like it or not. You have to love Him in order to get all your desires. He is your partner to success and you need to love and respect all the power He has. I'm sure you respect your president because you know and understand how powerful he is. Same should apply with God; in fact, you should respect Him even more than the president because He has the power over everything on earth and the heavens. When you work together with Him, you can achieve everything you need or want to be. All the power comes from within you.

A SERVICE BRINGS A SALARY: You just cannot work as a call centre agent and be paid like a call centre manager. The service you render will always match you rewards. Whatever you put in, is exactly what you'll get out. Doesn't the law say you reap what you sow? If you work harder today, you'll be paid more tomorrow.

OWN YOUR DREAM AND LIVE IN IT: Confirm and convince yourself by repeating your desires in your mind. Make sure that you own and live in your dream till it becomes a reality. You must be focused and nothing should ever take place in your mind expect your dream. Live in it and know that everything is in place and you are already living your dream. Repeat everything you write, talk about and visualise every time of the day till it takes place in your physical eyes. Own everything in your spiritual eyes till you obtain it in your physical eyes. **Discipline** your mind and never ever let your success get away.

EVERYWHERE YOU GO, TELL YOURSELF: Talk to yourself and say, I am super active; I do the best in everything that I do; I am healthy and getting younger each day. I attract good and loving people into my life. I am safe in this world. Tell yourself that every day is getting better and you are super rich. You must know that you are a millionaire already and nothing can ever stop you to be what you can think about. The fact that you can think about it, is the fact that you can achieve it.

MAKE SUCCESS ARE RECURRING THING: It's always best to think about the happiest moments in your life. Think about the time you past matric, the time you bought your first car, the time you bought your home, the time you had your first child, the time you got married and the time you got a present or won something big. Just think about any happy moment that has took place before in your life and just focus on it. It should bring back all the joy and happiness as you think about it and just live in that moment. This is the way that you should always feel and nothing should take place of this moment.

THE TREATMENT YOU GIVE WILL BE THE SAME TREATMENT YOU'LL RECEIVE: The treatment and focus you render in contribution to your dreams and goals will influence and calculate their treatment towards you. Make sure that you put all the energy that you have because you will get a reward for the effort you made at a later stage. You should program your mind to work for you at all times.

SURROUND YOURSELF WITH THE BEST: Do not settle for less at any time. You must know that you are the best and everything that you desire should be the best. Program your mind on only the best things, surround yourself with only the best, and make sure you become the best.

DON'T MAKE A MISTAKE: Remember that we are all connected. From one person, God made all nations who live on earth and He decided where and when every nation will be. Everything that you say to somebody else is being said onto you as well. If you don't want someone to progress and be successful, you are basically applying that onto your life. What you want for yourself should also be something that you would want for somebody else. This might be a challenge to some people, but don't have people that you love and some you hate. Just love everybody on earth.

HOW DO YOU CREATE PROMOTIONS FOR YOURSELF: This is simple, if you want a promotion to be present, just go into your mind and create one. Your mind is the creator of everything. Don't take your thinking abilities lightly, because you will limit yourself every time you think. Believe that everything that you think about will be made a reality, because it will really do. Every opportunity is created in your mind-set, so go on and think.

I HAVE FAILED, WHAT'S NEXT: This is the mind-set that you don't need at all. People don't fail in life, but they create challenges for themselves. Whatever you have created for yourself to take place, it's the same way you are going to take yourself out, since you are aware and conscious about everything. The greatest level of success is always after the action that you take after the considerable challenge that you faced. After my challenge I took action and it worked for me. You too can take action now and it will work for you.

THERE IS NO SUCH THING AS A PROBLEM, BUT A CHALLENGE WHICH CAME TO PROMOTE YOU TO YOUR NEXT LEVEL: I have come to understand that there is nothing in the world that is called a problem, but there are challenges which will come to promote you to your next level. It's up to you to decide whether you take the promotion or not, based on that you are also ready for your promotion. Most of them, if not all successful and wealthy people you know or read about today had to go through some challenges before they were promoted to the level they are in today. Going to prison was also a challenge to me, but a challenge which came with a promotion to the next level. It was up to me to accept the promotion by being ready for it. The truth will always remain that if I never had to go through the challenges I went through, it was never going to be possible for you to be reading this book today. I had to go through everything that I went through so I could talk about something that I know and personally experienced. If I didn't go to prison, where do you think a person like me who was addicted to drugs, alcohol and women was going to get the time to write this book which needed a lot of research? In the outside world there is not even time for a person who is not addicted to these things. Surely you'll be very busy with something else like the job you are doing, trying to acquire more money, and the time you'll spend with your loved ones, as well as other things to do. But the truth remains, life outside is too busy that you don't even know where the time went too, while you think you have enough time on your hands. So the challenge I went through activated one of my skills to the fullest ability and I received the promotion because I was truly ready for it. Through my challenges the secret was that I didn't see it as a problem as most people would, but I saw it as a challenge which came to promote me to my next level that was already waiting for me. I had to receive the position by being ready for it. It would be hard to explain something to someone while you not are fully equipped about the topic you want to talk about. And that's how you should also see your challenges in life. They came so you could learn from them and teach other people about what you personally went through. You created for them to take place in your life, and you can also create your way out as well. In my next book, I have a chapter which is speaking about this topic. This is where you'll see how you can make everything that has happened to you, work for you.

YOU REAP WHAT YOU SOW: You are told over and over again by the Law of attraction that like attracts like, and we are told over and over again by the Bible that you reap what you sow. Therefore, don't you see and understand that these two statements are corresponding? But it's that they are said in two different ways? Whatever you put in the ground to sow, you will also reap it. When you go to gym and exercise, you will reap the muscles and health, and you'll get exactly what you have sown. You can't tell me you'll get the muscles if you don't go to gym. Even if you take the supplements, they won't give you the muscles if you don't gym, but instead they will make your body very weird. Again it is said that, like attracts like. You just cannot tell me that you don't understand this very simple law. Whatever you sow and feed your mind today, is exactly what you will reap and get out tomorrow. The anger I buried inside me alive all these years from my childhood had to come out one day, and I ended up in prison. I was even lucky, as some people would say; that I got myself out with what I was thinking. Yet some people don't think positively and they really die in this place. Now I ask you, what have you sown in you over these past years? Will the outcome be outstanding or you'll be ashamed of the results? Are you even aware that what you have already sown in private will be taken out in public? Will you handle the outcome when it strikes you? Will you be even blessed like I was to take yourself out of the mess you'll be in? Why don't you just listen today and now, and take the advice I am giving you? You can alter and release your past now if you decide to listen. Take my advice and apply it. I personally never had a chance like the one you getting now. You are given a book to guide your foot steps and the choice is all yourself. I really didn't have all this information that you have now to pursue my life journey, and I had to taste what I had created with a life of somebody else. Again I ask you, what mess you'll be in tomorrow if you don't change your past now? Don't wait for the afternoon or the next day, but change now. You don't know what will happen tomorrow, but you'll know if you apply this book. They say if you want to go somewhere in life, it's better to ask the people who have been in that same road you are pursuing. All in all, I have given you everything that you need to know and the choice is **yours** from now onwards.

Chapter 15
FOUR EASY STEPS THAT WILL MAKE YOU RICH FROM TODAY

MAKE A LIST OF YOUR DREAMS: Writing down a list of all your dreams is setting them to take place. When you write something down it will always be there and every time you see what you have written, it will remind you where you should be. When you write something down and put it in a safe place, it's like speaking a word and placing it somewhere safe. Remember that a word that is spoken has a power to change everything.

MAKE A PLAN OF ACTION: Everything that you have written down will need an action plan, what steps to follow in order to achieve your desires. Remember that the action is everything and there has to be an action that is followed. Write down how you'll start in making your dreams a reality; when will you call, see or visit the person you need to see that will help you. You need to start taking action with this action plan and follow it.

HAVE A DEADLINE: Every time you do something, you need to have a finishing date before you even start working. Set a time frame that will be reliable to you and a time frame that you'll meet. This will allow you to work on time and finish your work on time. You can't work on something forever and that's why it is vital to have a time frame that will guide you at all times.

VISUALISE: Visualise and cast an image out into the future. Live in that image or spiritual world as if everything is taking place as it is. Don't miss or leave any details out of the picture you are creating. You can edit and add everything that you want to take place onto your physical world. This is the place where you really have to work hard on because this is a place where everything takes place and you really don't want to miss anything out. Focus and don't let anything disturb you. So go on and create your world with everything that you see.

What I have taught you here on this book needs practice and be applied. Learn to control your mind so everything will work for you.

Contacts

Email address: lungelothephoenix@classicmail.co.za

Facebook page: www.facebook.com/lungelothephoenix

Twitter handle: www.twitter.com/luthephoenix

Please email or write your testimonial on my Facebook page as soon as you experience change in your life. I would love to hear when the book helps you and how did it help you. Please also email or inbox me any questions that you have, or would love to discuss any matters with me. I can't wait for your feedback.

www.ingramcontent.com/pod-product-compliance
Lightning Source LLC
LaVergne TN
LVHW091249080426
835510LV00007B/178